Co-Dependency

*The Crazy Codependent in
Toxic Relationship –
The Codependency Cure,
Healing & Recovery from Trauma for
Emotionally Healthy
Love Relationships with
Partner, Parent, Mother or Father*

Margot Fayre

considered an endorsement from the trademark holder.

Table of Contents

Your Free Resource Is Awaiting

To better help you, I've created a simple mind map you can use *right away* to easily understand, quickly recall and readily use what you'll be learning in this book.

Click Here To Get Your Free Resource

Alternatively, here's the link:

https://viebooks.club/freeresourcemind-mapforcodependency

Introduction

The word codependency is very strange. Most words that start with the prefix "co" refers to something that has two or more components working together in a relationship. This word might have made more sense back in the 80s when it was used to describe the relationship between an addict and their partner, but things have changed.

If you took a walk around town and asked the first ten people you met what codependency meant, you would probably receive ten different answers or you may not get any answers. Codependency is a word that gets thrown around a lot, but very few people understand what it means, and yet, codependency has endured the times. It isn't a simple fad. It has moved beyond referring to addiction and has become something that will likely touch on you. Once you have made it through this book, you will understand the true meaning of codependency. You might discover coworkers, family, friends, and significant others hiding within these pages. You might even spot yourself.

The goal of this writing is to provide you with psychological insight mixed with self-help and personal growth. Most people will purchase books like these because they want to improve their relationships. If this is what you want to achieve, then you have come to the right place. You will get to see codependent relationships through other people's eyes. Then you will learn how to adjust your views so that you don't miss out on any of the important parts.

This book will go over what codependency is in all its forms. You will find out that codependency has the ability to exist in a person's mind and as a person's identity. These codependent relationships include those with substances, not just other people.

This book will help you learn about codependency and prevent yourself from becoming stuck in it. The following are a few of the ways that you will learn how to move past codependency:

- You will discover the real you and break the need for codependency.

- You will work with your partner to change.

- You will learn new skills, like journaling, that can help you.

- You will learn how to communicate in a way that doesn't require codependency.

- You will learn more about yourself through the use of the codependency quizzes.

You will learn how to embrace yourself and live for yourself. You will see your true value and no longer require anything or anybody else to give you worth.

Now, I do want to preface this book with a little about me so that you can understand where I am coming from. I was a codependent for much of my life, and I discovered this while earning my PhD in Psychology. This made me want to improve my life and remove the codependency and gave me my psychological field of study. That is what has brought me here today. I want to share with you my personal and professional thoughts and ideas for overcoming codependency.

Part One: Codependency

Chapter 1: What It Means to Be Codependent

The first appearance of the word codependency was in the 1930s. The term has since evolved through usage and practice to find a new place within our culture and common language. Like so many other psychiatric terms that have found their way into our conversations, such as passive-aggressive, dysfunctional, narcissistic, and paranoid, the meaning of codependency has become blurred through its move from therapy into the public domain. Codependency has changed a lot through its 75 years of usage, so it's important that people understand its usage history.

Psychological Theory

The 1960s created a lot of change and upheaval to the established way of thinking. The views on therapy for the mentally ill were no exception. This was when the beliefs about how psychosocial problems were treated, studied, and identified changed.

Codependency couldn't exist if an expansion of psychological theory didn't happen so that it included the elements of family systems theory, assertiveness training, the recovery movement, and the self-help movement. With these types of changes, it opened up the psychological world for new concepts and for old concepts to grow and mature. This improved their understanding of human behaviors. Codependency became one of these new concepts.

Codependency began life as part of recovery literature, which includes information for alcoholics or drug addicts. Today, it is more widely used in social work, psychiatry, and psychology. Therapists do work to help issues of codependency in therapy, but the DSM (*Diagnostic and Statistical Manual of Mental Disorder*), published by the American Psychiatric Association in 2013, which is a book used by mental healthcare professionals for billing, diagnosing, and treating mental illnesses, does not have it officially listed.

The Family Systems Theory

The term codependency is used to describe dysfunctional patterns of behaviors, beliefs, and emotions that are created from a person's inter-actions with their environment, especially within their family. Until family system theorists began their work, nobody had thought about looking anywhere but in the single patient's mind to see why they had their psychological problems. It used to be that a therapist saw one person and never thought about involving family members. This is the importance of systems theory.

The two main figures in family systems history are Murray Bowen, who was an educator, researcher, and psychiatrist, and Virginia Satir, who was a family therapist, social worker, and educator. During the 50s, these innovators were able to break from the established medical model and came up with a different way to view human behavior. Thus, the creation of the family systems theory.

The Revolutionary Change

Believing that a patient's psychological problems were connected with their family system was a revolutionary idea. As Satir discovered, no matter who is suffering from a problem, it is the existing conditions of the family system itself that will create and maintain dysfunction. At the time, this was a startling notion. It changed how psychiatry and psychology would progress in the treatment of psychological problems. With family therapy, the balance will shift, which creates a space for healing and allows the family members to change and find a new balance. This allows for recovery.

Alcoholics Anonymous

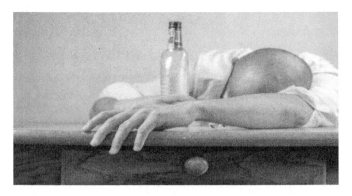

While Alcoholics Anonymous worked outside of the mainstream mental health system, it was the first group to identify codependency as playing a major role in alcoholism. During the 40s and 50s, the AA 12-step program popped up around the United States and around the world. In the early years of AA, they focused mainly on the individual, almost as if they lived within a vacuum. This is where the term codependent was used the most as a way to describe the spouse of an alcoholic. It could be that AA helped to influence family systems theory, or maybe vice versa. Regardless, both came to the same conclusion: The family was a big part in recovery.

In the early 50s, the revelation that alcoholism was a family disease appeared in recovery literature. However, it was years later that Melody Beattie would write her seminal book *Codependent No More*. This was one of the first books that provided readers with an in-depth explanation and exploration of codependency in an alcoholic family and was written in a way that the general population could understand. Beattie's work was able to illuminate and expand the concepts of displaced anger.

The Movement of Recovery

Now we have the distinct writings of Alcoholics Anonymous and family systems theory. They may have been written differently, but they were sharing the same message. Both of them validated the role of the family in the treatment of psychosocial ills, addressed the complicated interconnectedness of family relationships in keeping a disease or empowering recovery and focused on interpersonal relationships.

What we now refer to as the Recovery Movement includes not just AA but groups that also share the common belief of empowering people to recover within a group of peers. These groups exist along with professional mental health services and give aid to those dealing with parenting, divorce, grief, spending, depression, gambling, eating disorders, abuse, and so on.

While AA group meetings and their 12-step program started as the first treatment for addicts, AA also encourages people to get their family involved for inpatient treatment. AA has also started to create 12-step groups for adult children, teens, spouses of alcoholics, and codependents. This is moving us towards a family systems approach.

There is now a strong network of recovery groups that deal with many types of mental health issues.

Each of them has its own unique focus, but all of them still follow the format of AA.

What It Boils Down To

With the history of codependency and the realization that family plays a huge role in mental health, let's look at what exactly codependency means. Codependency is most often a behavior that is learned and passed down through generations. It is both a behavioral and emotional condition that affects a person's ability to have a healthy and mutually satisfying relationship. Some people even refer to it as "relationship addiction" since many codependents will often form or maintain relationships that tend to be abusive, one-sided, or emotionally devastating. Through years of studying how families of alcoholics interacted, researchers discovered codependency and the fact that it is learned by imitating and watching those around them who display a certain type of behavior.

Codependency has the ability to affect friends, siblings, parents, spouses, or co-workers of a person who is dependent on drugs or alcohol. Originally, the term codependency referred to partners in chemical dependency, people living with or dating an addict. There have been similar patterns found in people who are in a relationship with mentally or chronically ill individuals. Today, though, the term is now used to define any codependent person from dysfunctional families.

A dysfunctional family refers to one where members suffer from shame, pain, anger, or fear that is ignored or denied. Some underlying issues could include the following:

- The presence of another family member who suffers from a chronic physical or mental illness

- The existence of sexual, emotional, or physical abuse

- An addiction of a family member to gambling, sex, food, work, relationships, alcohol, or drugs

Dysfunctional families don't see that there is a problem. They won't talk about the problem or confront it. As a result, family members will often repress their feelings and ignore their needs.

They end up becoming "survivors." They create behaviors that will help them avoid, ignore, or deny difficult emotions. They try to detach themselves. They won't talk, touch, confront, feel, or trust. The development of emotions and identity of the members of a dysfunctional family tend to be inhibited.

They focus all their energy on family members who are addicted or ill. The codependent will sacrifice their own needs to care for the sick person. When a person puts another person's safety, health, and welfare before their own, they can end up losing contact with their own sense of self, desires, and needs.

Codependents will often suffer from low self-esteem and will try to find things outside of themselves to make them happy. They struggle to be themselves. There are some who turn towards nicotine, drugs, or alcohol, which causes them to become addicted. Some may form addictions to other habits, such as sexual activity, gambling, and work.

Codependent Behavior

They all have good intentions. They work hard to help others who are experiencing difficulty, but their caretaking ends up becoming compulsive and defeating. Codependents will often become martyrs and benefactors to another person's needs. A wife could try to cover for her alcoholic husband. A mother could make up excuses for their misbehaving child. A father could "fix things" for their child so they don't have to face the consequences of their delinquent behavior.

The biggest problem is that these rescue attempts give power to the needy person to continue with the destructive actions and to become more dependent on the also unhealthy caretaking of their benefactor. As their reliance increases, the codependent starts to feel a sense of satisfaction and reward from being needed. Once the caretaking ends up becoming compulsive, the codependent person feels helpless and choiceless in their relationship, but they can't break away from the behavior that has created this problem. Codependents see themselves as a victim and are attracted to this weakness in any of their relationships.

It's hard for them to recognize that they have a problem, while it may seem obvious to outside observers. They believe that they are helping a person in crisis. Initially, the codependent might set out to help the person work through their problematic behavior or addiction. Over time, though, this goal is likely not going to be reached. They adapt to the dysfunction and focus on maintaining the status quo. Just thinking about ending the relationship will cause them more pain than the thoughts of staying.

Growth of Codependence

Codependent behavior tends to be rooted in childhood. Children who were raised by abusive or uncaring parents may set aside their needs and start to follow self-sacrificing behaviors so that they can survive. If a child's parent or parents suffer from a mental disease or addiction that has gone untreated, a child may end up having to become the caretaker. The children of these situations are often considered to have been "parentified." Parentification refers to "the reversal of the parent-child role."

Since these children have been forced to grow up without their own developmental needs met, there is a chance that this could cause a cycle of codependency that gets passed down through generations.

It can be particularly harmful when it comes to parents of addicted children. A codependent parent of an addicted child can end up enabling their child's actions, even when they believe they are helping. The fact that parents who have addicted children are at risk of becoming codependent only proves how this concept of codependency has grown since the original framework of it only being the relationship between the spouse and the addict or the addict and their child.

Nevertheless, it doesn't necessarily come from the home. Children who have suffered sexual abuse may not be able to form their own sexual identity and satisfaction. This puts them at a higher risk of putting the demands and needs of a sexually controlling partner before their own.

Chapter 2: Codependent Relationships

Codependent people aren't always loving, nurturing, and passive. The peacemaker, the caregiver, or the woman who will give you the shirt off her back can all be codependent. Still, people who are cranky, resentful, angry, and manipulative can be codependent as well. If you take into consideration the main issue, codependent people rely on the views of others to let them know they are okay. You can start to see the importance of another's opinion. Take, for example, Blanche DuBois in the play *A Streetcar Named Desire* by Tennessee Williams. She relied on the kindness of strangers. This puts these people in a powerless position.

In the case studies that we are going to look at, you will get an idea of the different ways that codependency can show up in a person's life. People who are codependents come from various walks of life and are of different ages and lifestyles. You will also learn that codependency isn't just present in romantic relationships but can occur in all types of relationships.

The Alcoholic Sibling: Martha and Kenneth

Martha is a successful elementary school teacher in a small rural town. Her brother, Kenneth, is an actor living in New York City. Ever since they were teenagers, Martha has denied that Kenneth is an alcoholic. She has come up with excuse after excuse for him over the years. If at any point he appeared drunk on stage, she would brush it off as him working long hours and being tired. When he didn't appear for family reunions, she would say he was very busy. When Kenneth got a divorce, she said his drinking didn't have anything to do with it and told their family and friends that Kenneth's wife was cheating on him.

Whenever Kenneth calls Martha for money, she sends him some and hides it from her husband. When Kenneth gets arrested for assaulting a person during a bender, Martha tells her husband that Kenneth is sick and needs her help. She takes time off work and heads to New York City to be with him. She dips into her retirement to bail him out. While out on bail, Kenneth steals her credit cards and disappears. Martha's marriage barely makes it through this once her husband finds out what has gone on. Martha has a codependent relationship with her brother, Kenneth.

Helicopter Parenting: Jessie and Darla

Jessie is a single mom of her 15-year-old daughter, Darla. Jessie has referred to her daughter as "her life." Jessie often feels bad that Darla only has one parent, and she overcompensates by trying to keep Darla happy. When Darla looks the least bit upset, Jessie likes to give her things and do things for her. She works full-time, but Jessie has volunteered at her daughter's school since Darla was in the third grade. She was a Girl Scout leader until Darla dropped out. She currently volunteers for Darla's cheerleading squad and drives them to away for games. Jessie loves it when Darla talks to her about her difficulties, relationships, and triumphs. She gives her daughter advice and is upset when Darla doesn't follow it.

She has viewed Darla as "the perfect daughter," but her grades have started to fall recently. Jessie panics and meets Darla's teachers each week to talk about her grades. She gets Darla a tutor to bring her math grade back up to an A. Jessie has already taken it upon herself to send out for college applications and catalogs.

When Jessie sets up an appointment to talk with the principal about Darla's boyfriend breaking up with her, the principal refers to her as a "helicopter parent." Jessie leaves feeling unappreciated and angry.

Growing Old: Jan and Mother

Jan is the oldest of 10. She grew up on a farm in Nebraska. The entire family pulled their own weight to work the farm. Jan was 16 when her father died, and her mother relied a lot on her to help manage the farm after that. This caused Jan to grow up fast. Being a third-generation cattleman, naturally, she inherited the family farm and expanded to include crops.

All her brothers and sisters leave once they graduate, but Jan stays behind, marries, and keeps up with the family business. Her mother helps her raise her children and does the best she can by taking care of their garden, cooking, and canning. Jan's husband works another job and helps out on the farm. They are able to make it through lean times when everybody works together.

At the age of 60, her mother suffers from a minor stroke. Jan and her husband tend to her mother until she recovers. A couple of years later, she has another stroke. This one leaves her partially paralyzed. Jan's sister comes and helps for a few weeks and the other siblings chip in with the additional expenses for the physical therapy.

Then Jan's mother falls and hits her head, which leaves her unable to talk or walk. As usual, Jan says that she will care for her in their home. As her children move away to go to college, it becomes harder for her and her husband to care for her mother and run the farm. Her husband has been helpful throughout all of this, but he thinks that Jan's siblings need to be doing more. Jan doesn't want to bother her siblings, and she argues that her mom can't handle change.

Jan's mother's health continues to get worse, and her husband's pleas to talk to her family continue. Jan won't budge. In an act of desperation, Jan's husband reaches out to the local Commission on Aging. The therapist tells her that they should have a family meeting to talk about how the other siblings can help. Jan becomes angry when she finds out and chooses not to participate. Her husband goes ahead with the family session and six of Jan's siblings show. Jan doesn't want to inconvenience them, so she grudgingly goes.

The meeting helps, and her siblings say they will help in their own ways. Several suggest having their mom visit for a few months at a time. Two of them can pay for her daily needs. One says that he will take her to her medical appointments. Jan leaves feeling like a giant weight has been removed and hugs her husband, thanking him for intervening.

Then, the first time one of her sisters says they can only keep their mom for two weeks, Jan says, "That's okay." When her brother stops helping out financially, Jan doesn't feel right begging for money. Since Jan can't hold her siblings accountable, along with the need to take care of her mother, all the help she had falls apart.

Jan created a codependent relationship with her mother very early on. From then on, it was easy to continue with her pattern of codependency with her entire family.

Narcissism and Codependency

Let me share with you a joke a friend of mine told me when they discovered my study of codependency:

"Two codependents have sex. In the afterglow, one says to the other, 'Well, it was good for you, how was it for me?'"

Codependents don't have much in the way of a personal relationship with themselves. They put other people's needs before their own. This isn't the least bit healthy.

Narcissists also have a very unhealthy relationship with themselves. They place their importance way over everybody else's. They use other people to help their own needs and exploit all their relationships without feeling any type of remorse or guilt. They always blame other people and can't see that they had any hand in the wrongdoing.

With this, it's easy to spot how these two types find each other. There is an elegant dance going on between codependents and narcissistic types. They are like two puzzle pieces that fit perfectly. One is an easy victim for the other, though there also exists a deeper connection.

There has been a familial link found to this type of interaction. If a person was raised by a parent who is narcissistic, they are more likely to become codependent or narcissistic. If both parents are narcissistic, the same holds true.

As a person starts to recover from codependency, they will start to set boundaries and face the narcissist. Most humans find it difficult to conceive of a person who doesn't have the ability to empathize and learn from their past mistakes. The biggest mistake that codependents make is giving somebody the benefit of the doubt, especially when it comes to their narcissistic partner, because they find it hard to believe somebody could be so selfish. So, the cycle begins.

The great thing for a codependent person is that they can recover once they completely understand that the narcissist doesn't know how to have compassion, which is something that makes us human. Since codependents will often blame themselves for problems, they often find success with therapists. This isn't true for narcissists. They are going to be stuck within their own little world of non-blame, causing them to be unable to change. How can a person change if they can't see that they are doing anything wrong?

Chapter 3: Signs of Codependency

There are plenty of people out there who find themselves repeating the same unhealthy relationship patterns, despite good intentions. In fact, my own struggle with unhealthy relationships is what led to this book.

As we have discussed, the traditional definition of codependency revolves around the maintenance, control, and nurturing of relationships with people who are chemically dependent or engaged in negative behaviors. The classic model was the alcoholic husband and his wife.

In their 1991 book, *Children of Chemically Dependent Parents*, Dupont and McGovern stated that they believed that codependent individuals share responsibility in the unhealthy behavior, mainly keeping their focus on the sick or negative behavior and creating a connection between their wellbeing and the behavior of the other person.

Le Poire (1992) believed that the healthy individual nurtures the afflicted person when they engage in negative behavior. This is pleasant to the sick partner, which helps to reinforce the problem.[1]

In Melody Beattie's 1987 book, *Codependent No More*, she states that the partner that has the most control is seen as the powerful one, while the other person becomes indebted to them.

However, it takes two to tango. There is, in fact, an underlying agreement between the two individuals. The subservient or dependent person might not be as innocent, passive, or weak as they seem.

The following questions and signs will help you to spot codependency within relationships.

1. Do you often keep quiet so that you don't start an argument? The codependent likes to feel like they are making things easier for the other person. If any argument were to take place, that would mean they haven't done their job properly.

2. Do you feel that you are trapped or underappreciated within your relationship? A codependent person uses a lot of energy to take care of another person's life. All of this is done under the guise of really wanting to help the other person. When the person ends up ignoring or rejecting the advice, the codependent will end up feeling unappreciated, angry, and abused.

3. Do you worry about how other people view you? Codependent's happiness depends on other people. If others don't like them, then they don't like themselves.

4. Do you cover up the problems, like alcohol, drugs, or law problems, that your partner, friend, or a family member has? Since a codependent doesn't deal with their own

feelings directly, they come up with techniques to lie to themselves about how the other person is behaving. Since they feel that they are responsible for the other person's actions, they will blame others or rationalize things for their loved one's actions, or they even blame themselves for their actions in order to maintain control.

5. Do you find it hard to tell them no when they ask you to do something? The codependent fears failure and rejection and sometimes express these feelings. In their mind, they are unlovable. A codependent finds it hard to trust other people easily or share openly because they are afraid of being exposed.

6. Do you have to make extreme sacrifices to make another person happy in order to feel like you have a sense of purpose? Codependents will go above and beyond the call of duty to make others happy. They want to receive approval, love, or feel as if they are liked and accepted. If they don't

get the approval they want, the codependent will feel like the victim.

7. Do you feel responsible for fixing another
person's problem? A codependent person
feels like they have to solve others' problems. They believe that the other person
needs their help. They think that the other
person is unable to make the right choices
or take the right course of action to solve
their problem.

8. Do you often offer advice whether a person
asks for it or not? A codependent person
will jump at the chance to provide advice.
They can come up with an endless stream
of good advice no matter if they have been
asked or not.

9. Do you expect others to do as you say?
Once a codependent has given advice, they
expect their advice to be followed. Codependents don't understand what it means
to have boundaries.

10. Do you tend to take things personally?
Since there are typically no boundaries,

any action, comment, or remark reflects on the codependent. This creates the need for being in control.

11. Do you feel like you are the victim? Everything that happens to the other person or the codependent is a reflection on the codependent. These people will often find themselves feeling powerless and victimized. They are unable to understand their role in making their own reality.

12. Do you ever try to use guilt, shame, or manipulation to control the behavior of others? To get their way, codependents will act in such a way that will force other people to comply. These can be unconscious actions. This could be something as simple as giving them the silent treatment when they don't do what you want. You likely won't consciously realize what you're doing. Since others' reactions are reflections on the codependent, it's important that the codependent feels like they have the control.

It's not surprising when codependents turn to addictive behaviors to help them negotiate unresolved feelings. They use things like food, drugs, or alcohol to control their emotions, or they will partake in risky behaviors. When this happens, they can easily lose control. Their codependency and addiction will both worsen. Their physical and mental wellbeing will become impossible. The only way to resolve the issues at this advanced stage is through rehab.

Codependents magnetically and habitually attract other people who are not motivated or interested in participating in a reciprocal relationship. By constantly picking addicts or narcissists as friends or romantic partners, codependents find themselves feeling undervalued, disrespected, and unfulfilled. Even though they complain and feel resentful about the inequality in their relationships, codependents don't feel like they can change.

Chapter 4: Codependency Personalities

Just like there are different types of people, there are different types of codependents. These different codependents act in different ways, meaning you might not see certain codependent tendencies in one type, but you might in another.

A passive codependent tends to be avoidant and fearful when it comes to conflict. A passive codependent will often try to influence or control their partner using carefully executed strategies, most of which are supposed to go unnoticed. This is due to their fear of being alone, low self-esteem, and propensity to find themselves in relationships with dangerous, abusive, or controlling manipulators. Since they are secretive and hidden in their controlling natures, they are often seen as the more manipulative codependent.

Active codependents, though, are more overt and bold in their attempts to manipulate their partner into reaching their needs. They are not as afraid of conflict and harm, and they are more likely to start confrontations and arguments with their

partner. These types of codependents are sometimes viewed as narcissists since they are more
open in their actions. While they find themselves
in a never-ending cycle of working to control another person who isn't capable or interested in
meeting their needs, they still don't have the urge
to bring the relationship to a close. They fully believe, like the passive codependent, that they will
be able to "fix" the other person. It never happens, though.

While these types of codependents may have different outward appearances, both suffer from an
"others" self-orientation. They both tend to stick
with pathologically narcissistic or addicted partners while also feeling unhappy, resentful, and
angry with the lack of reciprocity within the relationship. The active codependent might come off
as stronger and in control, but both share a deeply
embedded feeling of insecurities. Neither type
can break free from their relationship.

Now, while we have the main two subcategories
of codependency, active and passive, those two
can break down further into five more subcategories.

The Martyr

Suffering is a virtue in the eyes of this codependent, especially when it comes to putting others' needs before your own. At least, that's what people might learn from their cultural heritage, religious institution, or family. At work, this codependent will always pick up an extra project and is the last one to leave, choosing to pass on drinks when a friend asks them. When they do go out, they will pick up the tab unasked even if they don't have the money.

When sacrifice makes up a person's being, it causes them to neglect their need for care and love. Ironically, that is why these codependents are always jockeying for the appreciation of others. This will often backfire. Not only will they start to resent those that they have helped, but the beneficiaries will either take everything they do for granted or start to resent the codependent as well. A martyr is often a form of active codependency.

The Savior

The world is scary. Fortunately, the savior is here to protect everybody. When their child faces problems at school or conflict, they are in the principal's office the very next day to work out a solution. When their friend can't make rent, again, they float them some cash so that she doesn't get kicked out.

Everybody will, at some point, need help. Although, when a person feels personally responsible for other people's wellbeing and comfort, they strip the other person of their chance to make their own wellbeing and comfort. The codependent enables self-limiting actions and basically sends them the message that they are helpless. Over time, the other person could end up believing this. This is a form of passive codependency.

The Adviser

If this codependent were one of the characters in the *Peanuts* comic strip, it would be Lucy. They sit at their makeshift desk providing people with advice about everything under the sun for a nickel. This type of person might have a great skill in seeing through other people's problems and offer clear options. They could also think that they have great insight into other people's problems. Listening might not actually be one of their strengths.

This is definitely one of the situations where it takes two. This type of codependent often views people who constantly seek advice as a person who doesn't have very high self-esteem. However, those who feel like they have to control and advise others are just as insecure. This is what is known as borrowed functioning. The codependent, who takes charge or tells others what to do, is just as needy. They need to have another person to let them be in charge to help boost their self-esteem. Both are dependent. This is a type of active codependency.

The People Pleaser

This codependent loves volunteering at their children's school and helping their neighbors fix their house. They like to make a coffee run for their coworkers. It's especially great for them when they can feel the love and bask in the praise of their generosity. Still, all this niceness comes with a dark side.

This dark side is reached when the codependent starts to feel like their gifts are no longer being appreciated or when the thoughts of throwing another party seem like a chore. It definitely has been reached when they start to use their people-pleasing skills to try and control those around them. They believe that others will like them for their favors rather liking them for who they are. This form of codependency is passive.

The Yes Man

This codependent will say yes to something even when they mean no and resent it. They plaster on a fake smile in agreement with their friends instead of telling them how they feel. They remain passive with their significant other and never tell them when they are upset.

Oftentimes, therapists will hear things like "We never fight" from couples in therapy. They look to us like we should approve of this, but what this tells us is that there is no honesty in that relationship. A total absence of conflict is not a good thing in a relationship. You can look at this from a business standpoint as well. When the majority of workers in a corporation are "fine" with their jobs and there aren't any complaints, it is because people are afraid of losing their job. The act of pushing away your true feelings, instead of finding a nice way to share them, is going to cause problems. This is a form of passive codependency.

Being a reformed codependent, I can see things in a different perceptive as a therapist than most. I understand where they are coming from, but I also know it's not healthy.

Codependency in Childhood

It's probably hard to imagine that a child would be considered codependent. Children form psychosocial problems from the time they are born. They respond to things and people around them from day one. Arguably, children are just developing their personality traits until they hit their teenage years, so it could be more accurate to say that early programming could end up resulting in codependency traits later on.

For example, let's look at the helper child, Julie. Julie is six and has become "mama's little helper." She wants to help her with the cooking, cleaning, and caring for her younger sibling, who is only 18 months. Her mom and dad thank her for all the help. The child will bask in this praise, especially when her mother tells her friends how much she appreciates Julie. "I couldn't do it all without her help," Mom says. Julie will sometimes be allowed to serve refreshments to the members of her mom's card club. Julie will then sit quietly while they play cards.

Julie's dad is very busy. When he gets home, Julie will take his shoes off and help him put his feet up to relax. She gives him the paper and a beer. He smiles and kisses her on the cheek. "That's my good little girl," Dad says as he leans back and opens his paper.

There are plenty of signs that single the development of caretaking behavior. Girls at this age should be playing with friends. A child is normally self-centered, and that is perfectly okay. That's how they develop their sense of self.

Of course, it's great for children to spend time with their parents as well, but usually, it's playing games, reading, talking about what happened at school, and so on. There is an unbalanced dynamic here. Julie is caring for her parents when they are supposed to be taking care of her.

Julie will outgrow this, but as she starts to separate from her parents and wants to play more with friends her own age, her mom will start to pout and say things like, "Who is going to help me take care of the baby?" This is when Julie hits the second phase of programming. She starts feeling guilty for normal childhood actions.

As she enters adolescence, Julie is more worried about how others view her. She becomes a "teacher's pet" and people-pleaser and continues to put her mom's needs first. Julie will end up being a caretaker and feeling responsible for others and never taking care of herself.

Codependency in Adolescents

The stage of development starts when a child hits adolescence. This stage typically lasts from age 12 to 18 or 19. This stage focuses on Identity vs Role

Confusion. The teenager struggles with fitting in and is working on figuring out who they are. They are creating close ties, figuring out how to interact in more intimate ways, and thinking about their morals. They are in the weird phase of not being a child and not being an adult.

Let's take a look at a type of codependent adolescent. Amanda is 15 and a sophomore. She hit puberty earlier than the majority of her friends. She was fully developed by 13. Suddenly, she looks a lot older than the girls her age, which causes her to receive a lot of attention from boys and some men. At first, she finds this terrifying. She feels like a child and is confused by this attention.

As a child, Amanda learned that she needs to get the approval and attention of adults. She has turned into a "pleaser." Her worth is dependent on noticing and tending to other people's needs. It began with her parents and then turned into her teachers and other adults.

With her new body and development, she has now discovered a new way to make people happy: sex. Amanda isn't even interested in boys in her class. She is more interested in fitting in with the popular girls, but they reject her. Nevertheless, boys seem to like her and being around her. If they ask for something, she wants to help them. Through sexual encounters, Amanda thinks that she has found approval. Only after does she experience guilt and shame.

Unfortunately, her attempts to gain approval cause her peers to judge her. Now she knows that there is no way the popular people will like her. She has reached an identity crisis. Despite trying to be liked, she sees others viewing her as unlovable and bad, the thing she wanted to avoid to begin with.

Amanda lacks an internal compass and the external judgments are detrimental. This could destroy her self-esteem. Now she feels hopeless and attempts suicide, which places her in the hospital.

The good thing is that Amanda is still alive, and there is always hope. With help before she completely solidifies into a personality, she might be able to continue in life without being codependent.

This road back is going to rough for Amanda, but with some help, she will be able to spot where she went wrong. Insights are the first step toward helping her discover her true self.

Codependency in Parents

Codependency is often passed down through gen-erations. If the unhealthy pattern lives in a state of unconsciousness, it can't be changed. How can something change when you are unaware of its presence? While moving through this awareness process, it's important that you don't feel guilty or self-deprecating when you start to realize that you have been a role model for codependent behavior for your children.

All a parent wants, or should want, is for their child to grow up in a good environment so that they can become a healthy adult. Parenting might be an amazing experience, but it's also a daunting job. It's also important to realize that there is no such thing as a perfect parent.

Let's take a look at an example. Janet and Ray got married straight out of school. They settled down and had two children. Janet's life has always revolved around Ray's. They moved across the country for his work, which caused her to fall out of touch with her friends and family. She felt she was living the "American dream." Ray had other plans. When Ray got his next promotion, he went without his family.

Janet was left with two children and no job. She was depressed and felt abandoned. She eventually got a job in a clothing store, but it wasn't enough to support her children. The savings she had from the divorce settlement didn't last long. Janet had to sell their house and move into an apartment. Being a single parent and having to work six days a week for minimum wage wasn't what Janet had planned on doing with her life.

Two years pass and Janet decides to find a new husband. She needs somebody to share the burden with, help take care of her children, and care for her. She pays a young girl down the hall to babysit the kids so that Janet can stop for drinks on her way home. Before long, she starts meeting men and going out.

What was meant to be a short-term plan to find a husband becomes a lifestyle. She loves this new single life, dating, and going out to fancy restaurants. It's like she is living a double life. Her dates don't know she has kids. Since she is in her 20s, she fits right in. The problem is, she doesn't fit in because she is not a young single.

When she meets Danny, he seems to be a perfect match, but he says that he doesn't care for kids on their first date. Janet chooses to wait and see if they fall in love before she says anything about her kids. For a year, the kids hardly see their mom. She gets up early to go to work and the babysitter takes over after school and puts them to bed around three times a week. Janet travels with Danny on the weekends. She leaves Friday night when she gets off from work and returns Sunday night once the kids are in bed. The children stay with an older woman in the building on the weekends.

First, the children are abandoned by their father, and now their mother is basically abandoning them. The worst thing they have to face is uncertainty on a daily basis. They talk to their mom on the phone to see what is going to happen. They beg her not to go out, but she hugs them and says she has to go on another adventure. The things they hear and the things they see don't match.

The codependency Janet had in her first marriage kept her from being able to invest herself in a healthy way with her husband. She was worried about being what he wanted her to be. Then her manipulative and dating behavior continues this pattern. Janet wants to find somebody, so she is willing to become whatever he wants her to be. Her relationship with Danny is about to reach the boiling point. She can't pretend to be childless forever. Janet has hidden them for months waiting for Danny to love her. Soon, he is going to find out and start to wonder who the woman he loves is. The really tragic part is the negative effect this has on her children.

Codependency in Friendship

Codependent thoughts and feelings are often only experienced within our most intimate relationships. This can cause subtle codependent behaviors, or they can cause crippling patterns. Codependency can be intermittent or chronic.

Take, for example, Catherine. She hasn't seen her friend Leslie since they graduated high school, but Leslie e-mailed Catherine, telling her she has gotten divorced and is moving to Sacramento, where Catherine lives. Catherine has lived there for 20 years now. Leslie tells her she's afraid of moving there, so Catherine offers to help her get adjusted and sets up a lunch date.

Catherine is waiting for Leslie when she hurries in. They hug, sit down, and Leslie starts complaining about the traffic. She hates the crowds and asks why Catherine didn't suggest a restaurant that was closer to where she lived.

Catherine warmly greets the server and knows him well. When he brings their food, Leslie is upset with her meal. She says the portions are skimpy. The server nicely asks her if she would like more bread or some soup, but the nicer he is, the angrier Leslie gets. Finally, she tells him to remove the salad and bring her a burger. She eats her burger but complains that it's "undercooked." During their two-hour lunch, Catherine has to listen to Leslie berate her ex.

Leslie calls Catherine every day asking for recommendations for various things. When they meet up, Leslie fusses about Catherine's suggestions. She is upset Catherine's dentist caused her gums to bleed. This lunch leaves Catherine feeling tense.

Catherine decides to invite Leslie to her holiday party. After the party, Leslie complains about the guests and how they were rude. Catherine listens for a while and then finds a way to excuse herself. Catherine starts screening her calls to avoid Leslie. Catherine's husband has begun to resent the negativity that Leslie has brought into their life.

Catherine knows this is true, but when she runs into Leslie, she makes excuses and feels as if she has to spend time with her. When they go to lunch, Catherine hides it from her husband.

Catherine can't create healthy boundaries with Leslie. At this point, she doesn't like Leslie, but she still feels stuck. Catherine is always stressed, even at home, because she never knows who is calling when the phone rings. She knows her husband is right, so now she is affecting their marriage. Catherine withholds information from her husband because he is the bearer of bad news. The bad news is Leslie thrives on anger and Catherine is a hopeless codependent with her and can't find a way to break free.

Chapter 5: How the Mind Works

Codependency is fear-based. It causes behaviors and qualities that are formed from feeling anxious and causes hyper-vigilance in intimate relationships. Here's how this works: when a person is scared, the left brain, which is the language center, becomes overwhelmed and stops working. Remember those times in class when you knew the right answer but couldn't think of it when put on the spot? The section of the brain that stays active, no matter how scared the person is, is the emotional part, the right brain. People keep their ability to be able to scan their environment and read other people's emotions even when they are completely terrified. When people are scared, these parts of their brain work overtime.

For example, a terrifying moment for a codependent is when they realize a relationship isn't working. Facing the dissolution of a relationship is hard for everybody, and it's natural for people to try to do something to keep things going. When it comes to a codependent, they go above and beyond what typical people will do to help a relationship.

This ends up leaving them feeling bitter, lonely, exhausted, resentful, and angry. This can cause them to become martyrs and complain about everything they have done without getting anything back. There are times when they go to extremes.

When the relationship ends, they will be overwhelmed with guilt and grief, and they might find themselves obsessing about what they could have done differently. They might even try begging again or try seducing them. These are all attempts to try and get things to work for them.

The following are just a few things that I have done to try to keep a relationship from ending:

- Became inconsolable

- Became depressed

- Pleaded or begged

- Threatened my partner

- Tried to make them feel guilty

- Stayed financially dependent on them so I couldn't leave

- Became seductive

- Wouldn't speak up for what I wanted

- Tried to find things we could do differently

It's very humbling to say I did these sorts of things, and it's an important part of recovery to take an honest and hard look at past behaviors so that things can change.

I learned from a young age that my actions in public places, school, or church would either embarrass my parents or make them proud. My compliance with religious rules had the ability to save my family or ruin everything. Without knowing what had happened, I created a subconscious belief that I had power over others. If I said and did the right thing, everybody would be happy and stay together.

Codependents also tend to be afraid of being abandoned or have been abused or neglected. When the worry of abandonment creeps up in a relationship, they will try everything to keep things together.

Triggers

The things that codependents react to, their triggers, are unique to each person's history and personality. Triggers can be viewed as wounds, which tend to come from past trauma. When triggered, the person is living through a past injury again.

Some triggers can be internal. You can trigger yourself into feeling ashamed if you can't reach the measures you have adopted for yourself. The inner critic can be activated and ruin your day. Since codependents believe they should self-sacrifice, when they are asked for help, it could trigger their automatic offer of assistance. Another common trigger is being told they are "selfish" or "too sensitive."

Then there are the external triggers and overreactions. Overreaction tends to happen when the duration and intensity of a person's feelings or behaviors are a lot higher than normal. Codependents often overreact when an external trigger causes them to remember an experience that they have had with somebody in the past. These are normally hard to see because they believe their perceptions are true. An overreaction caused by an external trigger can cause what a person really wants to avoid.

The most common triggers are:

- Being compared to somebody or being criticized

- Being put on the spot

- Someone is angry

- Being asked for something

- Seeing a person in distress

In the next section, we are going to look at some steps you can take to overcome the codependency we have learned about so far. And if you like what you've learned so far, or you've found benefit, feel free to leave a review on Amazon. I really appreciate it as your feedback means a lot to me.

Part Two: Overcoming Codependency

Chapter 6: The Road to Recovery

Ending your codependency must begin with you. You aren't the cause of the other person's addiction, so you can't fix it. You also have no control over what your loved one does. If you want to help others, great, but you have to get well first. After all, it's not possible to be there for somebody else when you aren't there for yourself.

Recovery won't be easy, though. Recovery means you will have to make a 180-degree reversal of your patterns so that you can connect with yourself. When you heal, you will develop the following:

- Congruent and integrated actions, values, feelings, and thoughts

- The capability of being intimate

- Autonomy

- Authenticity

The change will require four main steps:

1. Abstinence: This is the most important part of recovering from codependency. The goal for you is to turn your attention back to yourself. You want an internal "locus of control." This means the things that motivate you should be based on your feelings, needs, and values. You learn how to meet those needs in healthy ways. Right now, you depend on others and give into things in relationships. Instead of abstinence, you learn that you can detach, people-please, and obsess over others.

Through abstinence, you will become more autonomous and self-directed. If you were the subject of an abuser or addict, you might fear displeasing your partner. This can require great courage to break off this pattern of conceding your power. Perfect abstinence isn't necessary to see progress, and it's impossible. There will be times when you slip up, but as long as you turn your attention back to you once you realize this, you will be fine.

2. Awareness: Denial is the hallmark of an addiction. This applies to a drug addict and the person in love with them. Not only do codependents deny that they have an addiction, but they also deny their feelings and needs, especially emotional needs for real intimacy and nurturing. A codependent could have grown up in a household where they weren't nurtured, feelings and opinions weren't respected, and emotional needs weren't met. Over time, they learn how to ignore their needs and believe that they were wrong. Some people decide to end up self-sufficient or find comfort

through work, drugs, food, or sex. This causes low self-esteem. To reverse this, you have to become aware that they are happening. The biggest killer of self-esteem is negative self-talk. The majority of people aren't aware of the internal voice that often criticizes and pushes them.

3. Acceptance: A big part of healing is self-acceptance. This is a lifelong journey as well. People enter therapy to change, but they don't realize that the work revolves around accepting themselves. Ironically, before a person can change, they have to accept the situation they are in. The old saying goes, "What you resist, persists." You will learn more about yourself through recovery that will require acceptance, and life presents many losses and limitations. You will mature during this process. Accepting your reality provides you with possibilities. A change will then happen. You will discover new energy that had once been stagnated from fighting your reality. For example, if you had been feeling guilty, lonely, or sad,

you will start to feel compassion, self-soothe, and act.

Self-acceptance means you will learn that you don't have to make everybody happy. You will learn how to honor your own needs and know how to forgive yourself and others. This goodwill allows you to become self-reflective without becoming self-critical. You will be able to watch as your confidence and self-esteem grow. You will no longer allow others to abuse you. Instead of manipulative, you will become authentic and assertive.

To improve your self-confidence and self-esteem, start telling yourself that you're killing it. We all need pep talks from time to time and telling yourself you are doing great will boost your self-esteem. If you do mess up, remind yourself that mistakes happen and it's not the end of the world. Also, you should do some things that make you happy. Take a bath, do some shopping, or have a scoop of ice cream.

4. Action: Insight without action is only going to bring you so far. If you want to grow, your self-acceptance and awareness have to be accompanied by a new action. This means that you will have to take risks and move from your comfort zone. This could be speaking up for yourself, doing something new, traveling alone, or creating boundaries. This means that you will have to make internal boundaries by committing to yourself or saying "no" to the negative voice in your head that wants you to resume your old habits. Instead of feeling like other people must meet your needs and make sure you are happy, you will learn how to take actions to make sure your needs are met and do things that provide you with satisfaction and fulfillment. Every time you try a new behavior or take a risk, you will learn something about yourself and what you need. You will have a stronger sense of yourself. This will help to build upon itself in positive feedback.

Just so you know, words are actions. The words you use reflect how you feel about yourself. Learning how to become assertive takes some time and is probably one of the most powerful recovery tools. Assertiveness means that you know who you are. It means that you need to set limits. This means that you honor and respect yourself. You are the writer of your life.

With this information in mind, let's look at some things that you can do to help kick-start your recovery. Keep in mind, these are only the first steps that you should take. There is a lot more that you can do, and we will go through many of them in the rest of the book. The first step is finding yourself.

My Strengths

When you have spent your entire life using all your energy and time to help a loved one, you have likely lost touch with yourself. Your own identity has likely become lost in their problems.

Instead, you need to reflect on your own talents, personal value, and strengths. More importantly, you have to live your own life by positively using those qualities you have just identified. This will help you to reestablish your life and create a separate identity.

I fully realized I had lost myself when I allowed my boyfriend in college to distract me from my schoolwork to the point that I failed a huge test for one of my classes. I know a lot of people get distracted by their boyfriends and girlfriends in college but for normal relationship things like going out and the like. I wasn't distracted by those things. I was studying for said failed test one day, and he called me up and said his parents needed help moving. I knew I didn't have the time to help, but I felt like I had to, otherwise he would be upset with me. Looking back, he didn't demand my help, he simply asked by saying, "Do you have the time to help my parent move?" He wouldn't have been upset if I said no and explained why, but I couldn't do that.

What Makes Me Happy?

The other person you have been "helping" is likely too consumed in their problems to meet your emotional needs. When you are codependent, you focus on all the needs of the other person to make sure your emotional needs are met. This leaves your needs unmet by anybody.

Quit allowing yourself to be neglected. Take a moment to think about your own desires and needs and what you need to do to make yourself happy. Then, do something about them. Write them down, act on them, etc. More importantly, don't let your concern about other people's needs stop you from pursuing what makes you happy, so long as you are not hurting anyone or yourself.

My Goals

A side effect of you neglecting your own emotional needs to make sure that the needs of the other person in your codependent relationship are met is that your goals have probably been pushed to the wayside. You might not even remember what they are anymore.

Maybe you think that your goals have changed and now they all depend on the other person's happiness. No. Those are not real goals. At least, they aren't *your* goals. They are desires that have been shaped and tainted by your codependency. Your goals might end up making others happy, but just like your happiness shouldn't depend on anyone else, neither should your personal goals.

Without considering the other person in your codependent relationship, spend some time generating a list of goals. At this moment, what do you wish to achieve in life? What do you need to do to get there? Detail your goal and the steps to reaching it while only focusing on *your* wants and *your* needs. You can keep track of these goals and your progress for them in a journal as part of a written record of your efforts away from codependency, an exercise I will discuss further in another section.

My Finances

Like it or not, you have likely been helping your loved one with their finances. While you might not be buying the drugs or alcohol, some codependents do, but when you are financially supporting them, as in bills, groceries, and legal fees, it comes out to the same thing. They spend their money on their needs, and you spend your money on their obligations.

When you financially support a person like this, you could end up causing a messy financial situation for yourself. This causes more stress and worry. Nonetheless, when you make sure that your own financial obligations are taken care of first, you get rid of this stress and worry. When you make sure that your bills are paid and all your financial needs are met, you will feel less resentment, anxiety, and depression. This will also force the other person to take a look at their own financial obligations.

How to Engage with Others

As your codependency grows, you might notice that you withdraw from those around you. Guilt and shame will prevent you from asking others for help. Eventually, you will find yourself isolated, and the other person and their problems are your entire world.

However, when you are recovering, you will learn how to engage your mind and use your time in good ways. You will figure out how to interact in healthy ways with others, especially friends and family members that you could have started to ignore.

Don'ts

While some of these might seem to deal more with codependents of addicts, they can still apply to people who are codependent on anybody.

- Don't allow yourself to feel burdened by guilt and shame. If you are dealing with an addict, there are 24 million Americans out there struggling with substance abuse, you are by no means alone. Everybody cares and knows somebody who is addicted to something. The same is true if you are codependent on your children or aging relative.

- Don't waste your time nagging them. Everything that you want to say to the other person, no matter what their problems are, they have probably already heard somebody else tell them the same thing. They might have even told themselves that.

  If you constantly harp at them using the same old arguments, they will end up tuning you out and quit listening.

- Don't preach. Having a "holier than thou" attitude is only going to push other people away.

- Don't try to "fix" the other person. This is especially true when working with an addict. Once you allow yourself to realize that addiction is a disease that can be treated with professional help, the better it will be for the both of you. You can't cure them.

- Don't "control" them. There is no amount of threatening, arguing, or convincing that is going to compel them to act the way you want them to.

- Don't feel responsible for their actions and problems. You aren't the cause of anything they do. They make their own decisions.

- Don't stay where you are abused. 20% of abusers are addicted to drugs and 70% are addicted to alcohol. More than 90% of assailants have admitted that they used alcohol or drugs on the day that they hit their partner.

Chapter 7: Making Changes Within

Everybody isn't going to choose to make a call to a therapist for help with their issues of codependency. This book isn't advocating a one-and-done approach. If you want to work on your codependency with a partner, friend, or alone, this book might give you some tools that can help you. They can also help when used with therapy or in group therapy.

Journaling

You might have had a diary as a child. It might have been a small book that had a fancy cover with a small lock and key. Once you got to be a teenager, you might have written in a journal about your deepest, darkest thoughts, gossiped about your friends, and cried about your heartbreaks.

Now, while you are beginning your exploration of your codependency, it will be helpful to begin a journal. You can do it in any way that suits your needs. You can use your computer, a spiral-bound notebook, three-ring binder with paper, or an expensive leather journal.

The Vault

Your journal can be a vault where you keep track of the work you are doing on your codependency. It can be a place you come back to when you need to remember how you felt or thought about something or give yourself a pat on the back for the journey you are in one. Journaling is used often in self-help groups or therapy because they are proven to work. When using a journal, you don't have to wait for your next therapy session or try to call a friend. You also don't have to work around family obligations. Find a quiet place, get your journal, and write down all those feelings and thoughts that are important when they happen.

There are many people who are afraid to put their feelings and thoughts on paper. They're afraid that someone might find and read their journal. Adults who were abused during childhood might have anxiety about being discovered, secrets, and privacy. Everybody needs a private place to keep their personal things. You might have to keep your journal locked in your car, but it is still worth doing. As you work through some of your problems, you might feel more confident with privacy.

While you think about using a journal, you might want to try some of the ideas you find in this chapter. You have the choice to write in an organized, planned way or a free-flow, unstructured style.

Mindfulness

This term has become very mainstream in the past few years. It describes a way to focus on what you are experiencing in any given moment of your life without judging it. There is a lot of evidence that mindfulness is a great tool to help manage and prevent addiction relapse and physical illnesses. It can help improve quality of life, depression, anxiety, and reduce stress. Mindfulness is found during yoga, meditation, and other such practices that have roots in Eastern religions and Buddhism, but mindfulness can stand on its own as well. The wonderful effects that these practices offer have been firmly established from many years of research. In order to show how accepting mindfulness has become in our culture, schools are introducing mindfulness as part of their daily classroom routine.

Having a state of mindfulness is important when working with your codependency. It can take you away from all the distractions of your daily life. It helps you to understand yourself intimately, get rid of the negative talk going on in your head, and accept yourself for who you are. This practice can improve your overall happiness. It might create a place where your new insights and creativity can emerge and flourish. With the help of your journal, mindfulness could help you observe yourself and the way you are in the present moment. It can help your codependency by pushing you away from old judgments and blaming yourself. You might want to begin each session with a mindfulness exercise. You could take a moment to notice something with each of your five senses to put you in a mindfulness setting. You could also try my personal favorite, the self-compassion pause. You simply take a moment and place your hand over your heart, or give yourself a hug, and take a few deep breaths. While doing this, think to yourself, "I hold myself with compassion. I love and accept myself. I live in peace." Live in this moment of compassion and mindfulness for a moment and then release your hand or the hug and continue with your day or journaling.

Mindfulness and Meditation

Mindfulness doesn't have to be formal. It also doesn't need to take a lot of time. Techniques such as noticing your breathing, sitting quietly, and letting thoughts enter your mind without evaluating them as good or bad can happen in only a few minutes. When you become familiar with how this works, you can get into this state when you feel you need to for as short or long a time as you would like.

Meditation is the act of focusing your mind on an object, thought, or nothing. This is done in order to train your mind for mindfulness and to achieve mental clarity and emotional stability. Mindfulness and meditation go hand-in-hand. Meditation requires you to use mindfulness and it prepares you to be able to tap into mindfulness whenever you need to.

The following is a simplified meditation:

Have a seat on the floor. You may sit on a folded blanket or pillow. Sit in a criss-cross applesauce position just like a child would. Just make sure you are comfortable. Be sure your hips are higher than your knees. Put your hands on your thighs palms up. Place your index finger and thumb together. Keep your spine straight but don't be too stiff. Use the spine's natural curve. Keep your shoulder back slightly with your chin forward. Keep your eyes focused and open. Focus on the floor about six feet in front of you. Some people will have something to use as a focal point. If you decide to do this, keep the same distance of six feet.

Breathe easy and start noticing your breath. Don't focus too closely on it. Just breathe and allow it to happen. Place your attention on the environment and body. Just notice it. This meditation doesn't want to clear your mind. Thoughts are important to mindfulness. Notice these thoughts running through your mind like a ticker tape. See them but don't make judgments. If you become too involved with your thoughts, you will start to lose awareness. Gently bring yourself back and focus once again on your breathing. If you begin to breathe too fast, notice it and return it to a relaxed breath. The main goal is to be mindful of whatever is happening. There isn't any wrong or right here, just breathing.

You can practice this meditation for ten minutes. You can begin to lengthen your meditation time to 30 minutes or more with time. The amount of time you want to devote to meditation is up to you and it won't be wasted. When this becomes easy, you can do this anywhere you would like.

Anger: Silencing the Storm Inside

Healthy anger is just a small cloud that moves over the sun. You are the only person who can turn anger into a storm. When you add your provoking talk to this anger cloud, you could stir up a huge storm. Suddenly, you are Dorothy. You get swept away and swirl out of control. You are not even certain about where you are going to land. You can easily unwind if you can learn to change the thoughts that helped to make the anger. You have the ability to calm yourself if you feel anger beginning to stir. You can do this with mindfulness and journaling.

Anger and Codependency

There is healthy anger. Anger might signal a violation of a boundary. If somebody comes up to you and kicks you, it is reasonable to raise your voice. It is also understandable that you insist this person stops kicking you. The unreasonable anger is what causes you to stop enjoying your life and causes you to destroy relationships.

Codependent people usually have anger, resentment, or rage problems since they are constantly looking for disapproval. They might become honed into their partner, who has become their ego mirror. They brace for rejection, constantly on edge, wondering if they are okay. If they get confronted with an image that isn't perfect, they might get angry and bully a person into silence or make them change their mind. At times, anger will fuel comments that aim to punish their ego mirror for bad impressions.

When you can accept the fact that anger is made by you, you will be well on your way to recovering. It doesn't matter if anger is outwardly expressed or simmers deep inside you in the form of resentment, it will affect your peace and keep you away from people that you care for and love. Rage is very destructive to anyone around you and yourself. It is extremely important for you to master your rage. Just like any feeling, anger is based on intensity. It can run from mild irritation and frustration to full-blown rage. Codependent people are usually angry since they are constantly trying to control others. This is something that will never be achieved.

Watch for Clouds Gathering

A good way you can utilize the body-mind connection when trying to reduce anger is regularly doing exercises such as running, walking, and swimming. These activities could help you identify a "zone" of wellbeing. Making physical balance a part of your everyday life will reset a trigger for anger.

It would be like walking on sharp rocks. This makes your body tentative and tense and makes you brace for injuries. The littlest thing will set you off when you are in this state. When endorphins kick in and you have a relaxed mind, you feel like you have entered a beautiful meadow that makes you feel comfortable, trusting, and relaxed while walking. The occasional tickle of grass is enjoyed rather than felt.

Other ways to achieve inner peace is by practicing Zen techniques such as mindfulness, massage, guided imagery, tai chi, yoga, breathing, relaxation techniques, and meditation. If you learn how to do some of these techniques daily, you can change your anger threshold. You can write about your Zen experiences when you journal.

Mindfulness can help on the front lines, too. Body sensations will give you your first clues to anger rising. Your heart rate will increase, your breathing will become shallow, your jaw will clench, muscles will tighten, your voice will rise, tendons in your neck will begin to stand out, and your eyes will either widen or narrow. Write these signals down in your journal. When you feel a warning, you need to take a break and practice mindfulness until you have calmed.

It might be helpful to get some assistance from a partner or friend when working with anger. Your partner will be a great help since they already see changes in you and can sense your anger before you do. A partner will change their position from enemy to friend. Pick a time when you usually don't feel angry. Agree to do an intervention where your partner will tell you if they see you getting angry. Remember you asked them to do this so you can't get defensive about what they say. You need to agree to stop right then and there without questions and take a break to do a meditation and bring yourself back to mindfulness. Once you are calmer and can use correct communication skills, return and resolve the problem.

Never Seed Clouds

Your journal is going to be helpful with this practice. Begin by listing everything you are mad about right this minute. Take the list and see if you have been trying to control something or someone that you don't have any control over. Delete them from the list. Look at what you have left. Do you have control of some sort over these but can't change them because of some positive action you have to take? Delete these. Look at the remaining items, which ones can you act on but you made a choice not to? Delete these.

Of the things that are left, stop and ask what the motivation is for your action. Will acting solve the problem? Will it help the friendship you have with the others involved? Basically, you have to make sure your heart is in the right place rather than just trying to be dominant. If your heart is pure, plan and act as quickly as you can. This should get rid of the list you made. If you have crossed out items, let them go. You can't do anything about it. You are the only one that suffers from the anger. Forgiveness and letting go will benefit you. Understand that getting the upper hand on anger isn't going to be as simple as deleting the item from a list. The way you deal with anger has been a habit that has formed over your lifetime. You might have even accepted your anger as just another part of you, but it is not. You might even try to justify your behavior by thinking that if you are angry, you are supposed to act badly. This isn't healthy. Since codependents look at themselves as the victim, they feel self-righteous about expressing rage.

Every day when you notice you have an angry feeling or you are actually getting angry at something or someone, never seed the clouds. Practice the techniques in this chapter. Make a list and give yourself the power to solve the problems without getting angry. This will be an ongoing process until you have gotten control of your anger.

Making Yourself Angry

This is another great exercise. Write the provoking self-talk down in the journal. These entries will show you in black and white the way you make yourself angry. Using just one or two sentences, record the incident that made you angry. Now, create a line down the center of the page. On the left side, list all the self-talk that fuels your anger. Once you have finished, write down a statement that counters the statement on the right side that might help lessen your anger. For example:

Mark is angry with Michelle because she has overdrawn their checking account again. This conflict has been happening during their whole relationship. He used to get very angry, self-right-eous, and accusatory when he found the account overdrawn. Let's see how Mark can start working on the problem. He draws two columns in his journal. The first column is going to show his anger-inducing self-talk. The second column, he will think about a way to talk that will lessen his anger.

Left Column

- She never listens.

- I work hard for our money. All she does is spend.

- She never cares about what I think.

- She is very selfish.

- She purposefully does these things.

Right Column

- She is busy.

- She also works hard. I spend the money, too.

- She might need some help.

- We are partners in this. Are there things I can do?

- Our method isn't working. How can we fix it?

This technique will give you a lot of information about yourself. There will be people who always believe someone else "made them angry." Can you see how this fits into the codependency category? Blame gets motivated externally. In order to change codependency patterns, you have to be motivated internally. You have to know why you do the things you do, why you feel how you feel, why you know what you know, and then use that information and act on it. You can't do it the way you react to the real world.

Melting a Cold Heart

The same techniques could help you be the kind of person you were before all the resentment, anger, and hurt turned your heart cold. Realize the things you do as you move through life doing whatever it is you do. Is your mouth turned down, brow furrowed, face tight with tension? Look in a mirror. How do you look? Discontented or mean?

If you can remember a time when you were a child and you felt cranky, your mom might have told you that if you didn't change the way you looked, your face would freeze in that position? You know that wasn't true, but our bodies hold onto memories. When you are outdoors on a sunny day, listening to music, taking a walk, looking at nature, if your resting face looks mean, you've probably had that look too often throughout your life. The codependency traits of trying to be all things at all times, over-functioning, inflexibility, high standards, being disappointed in what others said or did, trying to please others, and self-doubt are frustrating and exhausting. These can affect your wellbeing.

Use your journal. Jot down times in your life when you felt safe, secure, loved, warm, content, peaceful, excited, tender, and loving. You need to remind yourself that you have the capacity for true love. Now, use these times during this exercise. Do these as often as you can.

Pick a quiet space where you will have privacy and won't be interrupted. Pick a joyful moment from the journal. Now, close your eyes and recreate this moment. For this exercise, you put down a time when you held your baby for the first time. Remember the color of the blanket, who was in the room with you, how the baby's face looked, their small feet. Let yourself feel the joy. Notice the way your face changes, how your muscles and breathing changed.

If you are having problems with your significant other, think of a time when you felt close and loving to them. Let all the bad feelings go and let all the resentment and bad things you are holding in your heart melt away. Let yourself get into this experience. After doing this exercise, write down all the things you ever loved about your significant other in your journal. When you feel distant from them, try a short meditation before speaking with them. If you need a guided one, you can find many on the Internet. Try to find one that focuses on love and try to reconnect to the love you once had for your partner.

If you want to truly feel better both on the outside and inside, do these practices daily. The most debilitating part of codependency is being disconnected with one's self. Whatever you can do to connect and remain connected will change how you look at yourself and it will, with time, empower your life.

Chapter 8: Putting an End to Codependent Relationships

If you were to draw a series of rings and put a person in the middle, each ring that expands from the middle to the outer edge are people who have influenced them. The ring closest to the center represents the people who have the strongest influence on them, such as their children or partner. This makes them care about how their family feels, the way their family behaves, and what their family thinks. Somebody who is codependent relies very heavily on how their partner influences them. They don't just care about what their family does, feels, or thinks. They need their family to define who they are. Their partner turns into their ego mirror. They become a person that they count on that shows them their self-esteem and value. The bad news is this mirror doesn't have any grey areas. It will reflect in either pure white or total black, meaning they are either perfect or damaged.

Ego Mirror

This term is used to describe one person or several people who get used by a codependent person as a substitute for the way they view themselves. People who have intact, well-formed identities don't need to have an ego mirror. They completely know themselves inside and out, not the way they get reflected from someone else. They readily listen to people whose opinions they value and whom they care about. Anyone else wouldn't be able to rock their foundation by having conflicting needs, judging them, or disagreeing with them.

A codependent person's identity can be very brittle and shattered easily. This is why they are so desperate to change any negative feelings, whatever the cost. They have no idea how to change themselves on the inside, so they have to change their outside. If push comes to shove and they have to break the mirror, they will not hesitate to do it. Until that point comes, they will use any and all weapons at their disposal to force their partner to get rid of any concerns that might show they are not perfect.

A codependent person doesn't have the freedom to allow other people to be who they are. They can't stand to see another person angry with them. They can't stand for anyone to think badly of them or be disappointed with them. They are forever tied to a specific reflection. They are in a painful place because the only way for them to feel good about themselves is to make sure their mirror reflects them well.

See how you answer these questions:

- Are you constantly desperate that your partner understands your point?

- Can you stand it if your partner gets mad at you? Do you try to change their feelings?

- When you are in a deep discussion, do you always try to figure out how your partner feels before you share your feelings?

- After you have expressed opinions that are the opposite, is there a way you can agree to disagree with them?

- Do you get anxious if your partner ends or walks away from a discussion before the conflict gets resolved?

- If you get criticized by your partner, is there a way you can listen to it without explaining yourself in many different ways?

- Are you constantly aware of your partner's moods all the time?

- Can you take your partner's advice and think about it without getting defensive?

- Do you get uncomfortable if your partner asks you what your opinion is without giving theirs first?

- Do you give in to the needs of your partners and then get resentful?

- Do you feel panicked if you think your partner is mad at you and you can't figure out why?

If you said yes to just one of these questions, get your journal and write about it. Think of a time when you reacted that way to your significant other. Figure out if you can understand why you talk them out of the way they feel, why you always try to convince them of your position or have to have their approval. If you want your significant other to approve every action, feeling, and thought, you might be using them as an ego mirror.

Ego Mirror, Codependency, and Guilt

A codependent and a narcissist, at their core, will lack the same things. They don't have a healthy identity. Beneath the narcissist's bravado is someone who needs everyone else to validate their ego. Their ego mirror has to show their "the world revolves around me", "better than thou", and puffed-up sense of themselves. If they see inadequacies, imperfections, or faults, the mirror is wrong.

Narcissists don't feel guilty since they don't normally have identity conflicts. They are fine with their idealized self. They just need their ego mirror to shine pure white at all times. If the mirror doesn't give them this, they will try to find a new one. A narcissist's reflection would look like a perfect diamond, but unfortunately, it is only glass.

A codependent's identity looks like a flawed gem. It will have cracks, its color might be a bit off, and it has blemishes. This doesn't mean they are undesirable; they just aren't perfect. One diamond is just as shiny as any other diamond, but a codependent knows it has flaws. They have conflicts because they know the flaws are there, but they can't accept them. They have to have an ego mirror that shows their brilliance and doesn't show their flaws.

To quote Elizabeth Kubler-Ross, "People are like a stained-glass window. They sparkle and shine when the sun is out, but when darkness sets in, their true beauty is revealed only if there is light from within," as written in *The Leaders Digest: Timeless Principles for Team and Organization* by Jim Clemmer.

A person with a healthy ego and positive self-esteem will accept their imperfections and other's imperfections. A codependent can't. They will never accept their flaws and will work extra hard to deny them. They want to see themselves as shiny and possessing great qualities all the time. They try to be the most thoughtful, loving, considerate, helpful, and selfless human being. If they realize they aren't, they begin to feel guilty. If they see their flaws in the ego mirror, they won't be able to accept it, even if they know it is true. Rather than looking inside themselves, they will attack the mirror.

Guilt That Is Misdirected

When you think about codependents, you know they have an unrealistic sense of self. Their behavior might not match with their distorted self-image. If this happens, they will blame their ego mirror. The goal, though, is for interdepdence, especailly when it comes to friendships or relatiosnhips. Interdependence means that you rely on each other instead of one relying soley on the other. For example:

Lee and Jo-Ann have been with each other for 22 years. Jo-Ann is turning 50 and was diagnosed with multiple sclerosis. Jo-Ann's doctor meets with them and talks about the changes they can expect with the disease. He takes a lot of time with them, helping them learn how the illness will change their lives.

Jo-Ann has always worked hard and is now going to have to limit activities to keep herself healthy. The doctor asked Lee to make sure Jo-Ann didn't overdo it. He asks them to sit down with each other and adjust their chores to help with Jo-Ann's illness. Lee assures the doctor that he supports and understands Jo-Ann totally. He is happy to take on more chores.

One week later, they get around to sitting down and talking. Lee agrees to do all the chores while Jo-Ann does more sedentary work like cooking, dealing with phone calls, and paying bills. Whenever their friends ask how Jo-Ann is doing, Lee always points out that he is doing all the chores, is taking care of her and makes sure she isn't doing too much.

The truth is, Lee stopped doing the chores after a few weeks. From then on, he only did things after Jo-Ann asked him to and he didn't do them happily. Jo-Ann is having a hard time with her limitations and it is hard for her to ask for help. In several months and after the house begins to look like a pigsty, Jo-Ann can't stand it and asks to talk with Lee about the chores.

Jo-Ann: "Honey, I feel unnerved by the way the house looks."

Lee: "What do you mean?"

Jo-Ann: "It's filthy."

Lee: "Oh, for God's sake, Jo-Ann, it is fine."

Jo-Ann: "No, it isn't. The toilets are permanently stained, there is burned-on grease on the stove that I can't get off, and there is something that reeks in the refrigerator. There are cobwebs and dust everywhere."

Lee: "You are such a neat freak. You can ask any of our friends and they will tell you that you have OCD. No one expects a house to be as clean as you think it should be."

Jo-Ann: "You think my standards are unreasonable?"

Lee: "Yep."

Jo-Ann: "You said you would keep the house just like it was before."

Lee: "Don't you think that is a bit ridiculous?"

Jo-Ann: "No. That is how we have lived for more than 20 years. Our house has always been clean and tidy."

Lee: "And you don't think it is that way now?"

Jo-Ann: "No."

Lee: "Nobody in the world can ever please you, Jo-Ann. You are way too fussy."

Jo-Ann: "It totally bothers me to see the house this dirty and you keep telling me not to do anything, but you aren't following through with the agreement."

Lee: "Why do you always have to be so mean? You should listen to yourself. I wish I had a recording to play back to you of the way you talk to me."

Jo-Ann: "Fine, never mind."

Lee: "That's right. Clam up like you always do. Why do you always get to end the discussion? You are mean. I'm going upstairs."

Lee's identity of himself is one where he has to meet all of Jo-Ann's needs, and it isn't realistic. Lee doesn't want to admit that he isn't perfect. He would rather make agreements that are based on this idealized self. He tells everyone that he is Superman, and there is a small part that actually believes him. When his ego mirror Jo-Ann doesn't reflect him as perfect, he attacks her. This has been happening for 22 years. Jo-Ann has learned how to avoid conflict. If she does all the chores, never complains, there won't be any problems and Lee can believe that he is perfect.

Let's assume that Lee is journaling and trying to stop his codependency. After he storms out, he takes the time to experiment with a mindful exercise. With this, he can see his behavior and doesn't make harsh judgments. Since his self-esteem isn't at stake, he asks himself what he should do differently. Is there a way he can stop being defensive and let Jo-Ann feel the way she feels? How could he respond as a significant other who is in a relationship that is interdependent? He knew he dropped the ball on the chores, and he feels guilty. He gets mad at Jo-Ann rather than acting like a significant other who genuinely cares. Jo-Ann is Lee's ego mirror. Lee attacks Jo-Ann and walks out. Is this the kind of partner he really wants to be? He writes in his journal about it and then goes back to the kitchen to talk with Jo-Ann.

Lee: "Honey, I am really sorry about the house. You are right. I know I've said there isn't anything I wouldn't do for you, but I dropped the ball on the chores. I know you too well to know that upsets you."

Jo-Ann is beginning to cry: "I should have said something sooner before the house got so bad. I expect too much because it is hard on me being so weak."

Lee: "I want you to know you aren't expecting too much, but I might not be able to keep my end of the commitment in a way that will make you completely happy. What if I pay for someone to come in once a week to clean? I promise to pick up all the dirty clothes on the floor and do the laundry.

I just can't seem to find the time for everything else."

Jo-Ann: "That would be great. Maybe we could even have some time to hang out or go to the beach?"

Lee: "I'd love that."

Lee was able to notice that he didn't handle things well and was able to come back and resolve things in a healthy way. Being able to step out of your codependency and see where you may be overreacting is a great way to improve relationships with others and yourself.

Don't Look at the Mirror

This journaling exercise will help you turn away from the ego mirror. Your goal is to let your ego mirror quit their job. Let them be themselves, have their own feelings, beliefs, and reactions. It will be painful for a person to do time being a prisoner of your codependency. They can't be honest. They walk on eggshells just waiting for another meltdown or a blow-up. There isn't a way that they can be real when they are with you. Because of this, the two of you don't have a relationship that is based on interdependency. Interdependency is where the people in a relationship rely on each other instead of one person taking care of both. They work together. They help each other. One person doesn't take advantage of the other.

Write in your journal each day to record your thoughts and feelings. Draw a line down the middle of the page. Write down your codependent self-talk. Now counter that with interdependent self-talk. You have to know what the deepest problem you have to fix is. Since you are working on your identity, it will be worth all the work.

Here is an example:

Codependent

- Why in the world did he get so mad? Yes, I forgot to put the power bill in the mailbox. I didn't do it purposefully. He is just too rigid. He is a jerk.

- She is overreacting. Why does she get upset about every little thing?

- How could they be that mean? I worked for hours on that dinner and he didn't say anything about it. He will eat beans from now on.

- They are never satisfied with anything. I fold the laundry wrong. I bathe the children and do it wrong. I have had it with their criticism.

Interdependent

- I said I would mail the power bill and I forgot. I am not perfect, but I do need to apologize and find a way to learn how to be more responsible. I would love for him to be able to count on me. Maybe I should start writing things down.

- She was very upset. I should have helped her with the dishes. I should step up and stop being so blind to everything.

- I can tell he is enjoying the dinner, but I have to hear it. I'll just ask him if he likes the chicken.

- They have a problem with being a perfectionist. I like how I do things. Being a good dad and partner is up to me and I am very proud of myself.

It is fundamental to work on this part of codependency. The main goal is to know yourself and stop letting others define you. Use emotions to explore yourself. Big deal, your partner got angry just because you didn't do something the way they do it. It got done, that is all that matters. This doesn't mean you did something wrong. Even if you did it wrong, this doesn't make you bad. Let your partner feel the way they need to feel. Acknowledge their feelings and move on. You are still fine.

Setting Boundaries

You know that there is a difference in how codependents think they should be and the real them with all their flaws. Due to this, a codependent person isn't always going to be honest. They might make promises that are unrealistic since they think they should and not because they want to. They don't think it's fine for them to ever say no.

At times, deep codependency can become an unending cycle. You might hear things like:

- "If I were a better neighbor, I would help."

- "If I were a good husband, I would spend my weekends on fixing the house."

- "If I were a good son, I would ask my parents to move in with me."

- "If I were a good dad, I would get a loan to pay for my child's tuition."

It isn't possible to be everything to everyone all the time. Because of this, a codependent will let people down, and this, in turn, makes others angry. To their horror, they are then seen badly, and this reinforces their poor self-esteem.

Assertiveness

A good way to help you set boundaries is to practice being assertive. You will do it first in your journal and then in person. You can take time to write about whether you feel assertive when you have to deal with your partner. Assertiveness in this capacity is describing a way to set boundaries or being able to tell someone "no" in a way that isn't argumentative or aggressive. It also shouldn't be vague or tentative. It is a way to deliver your message that is direct, firm, and kind.

Do you have any of these illogical beliefs?

- My spouse will leave me if I let him down.

- If someone needs something, I must give it to them.

- I can't bear the thought of hurting anybody's feelings.

- My needs aren't as important as other people's.

- If I'm not generous, people aren't going to like me.

- If I don't help, people will think I'm selfish.

- I am being unreasonable if I don't do this or that.

While working on being assertive, use the journal to write down instances where you have agreed to do something that you actually didn't want to do and you resented it later. Put down what was going through your mind when you made the agreement. Try to get rid of all the "should" that was controlling the decision. Figure out what created the need to please, fear, or guilt. Figure out what you were thinking, feeling, and doing that caused you to agree to something and then later regret it.

For every incident you can remember, figure out an assertive way you might have set a boundary. Write as many responses as you can for every situation. There might be a time when you were caught off guard by a request. Be sure that you have different assertive statements you can easily remember and use when needed.

You can use some of these examples to begin your list:

Son: "Could you bring me my notebook? I forgot it in my room."

Mom: "I'm sorry. I hope you can do without it. I don't have time to bring it. I am completely covered with work today." (You don't need to get angry, whine about it, or blame him about how inconsiderate he is being.)

Husband: "My mom called, and I invited her for dinner tonight."

Wife: "I would love for your mom to come to dinner. It just can't be tonight. I'm not feeling well."

Wife: "Can you stop and pick up some wine for dinner on your way home?"

Husband: "Sorry, not tonight. I am just too exhausted."

Daughter: "I need the car tomorrow for school."

Dad: "Bad timing, dear. It is my turn to do the carpool."

Now try to think of some intimate situations where you might need to set some boundaries with your partner that might be hard to do.

Wife: "You have been on my mind all day. The kids are at the movies with friends. We are all alone."

Husband kisses her: "That is a great turn-on, honey. Is it possible to get a rain check? I am exhausted tonight."

Wife: "Do I talk too much?"

Husband: "Sometimes, but I still love you." (Gives her a hug and a kiss.)

Girl: "Will you come to my house to meet my parents on Saturday?"

Boy: "I am not ready, maybe sometime soon."

The above examples seem to be easy, but in all actuality, they aren't. The people who are closest to you expect you to automatically say yes. They won't understand this new you, and they will feel unpleasantly surprised. You might want to let your older children and your partner know what you are doing, that you have been working on improving yourself. Once they experience it, they will understand more.

When you start working on telling people "no" when you need to, just remember the main factor is if you feel or might feel resentful later. If you might, saying yes will make you dishonest and might eventually have a negative impact on your relationships.

It won't be long before you start to understand your true self while working through your codependency. If you can learn to be honest with yourself, your responses will be more honest as well. While learning all this, if you realize you have agreed to something and they see that you actually don't want to do it, you can go back for a "redo". You could use the examples above and imagine you have said yes, but you want to change your mind. Here are some examples:

Wife: "Will you run to the store for some apples?"

Husband: "Sure, what kind?"

Husband comes back ten minutes later: "Honey, I know I said I would go for apples, but would it be okay if I finished watching the game first?"

Daughter: "Mom, can you trim my hair today?"

Mom: "Sure, I have some errands to run first."

Mom comes back an hour later: "Debbie, I know I said I could trim your hair today, but I just don't have the time. Can we do it tomorrow morning?"

There will always be two sides to every coin when dealing with codependency. They will have problems setting boundaries. If a person sets a boundary on them, they can easily become angry or hurt. They are equally critical of others and themselves. They expect a lot from other people because they expect just as much from themselves. Since they don't have a solid identity, codependents react quickly to what they think is judgment. They see themselves as victims when others mistreat them, and they often feel disappointed or let down. It is hard for a codependent person to see others as being separate from them, especially their ego mirror. They don't think others should have their own behaviors, thoughts, and feelings.

Codependents tend to make everything all about them. They will react quickly when they think someone is being critical of them.

All the traits you can now see in yourself and the way you interact with your ego mirror can change with some effort. Use the strategies you have learned from this book and see a therapist if you think you need to.

Quick Tip: Write in your journal some positive affirmations and read them to yourself every morning and before going to bed. Delete the one that you have accepted as true. Add more to the list if you need to. In addition to the ones you come up with on your own, you might want to buy a daily affirmation book that has quotes from other people to keep on your nightstand.

To help get you started on your affirmations, here are a few that you can write down on a regular basis:

- I am worthy and good to me for me.

- I feel appreciate today.

- Today I view my childhood without shame.

- I am loved and I deserve love.

- I am a loving person.

- I am a strong and capable person.

Writing and saying affirmations help to rewire the brain so that you learn to focus on yourself instead of others.

Chapter 9: Improving Code-pendency in Life

The hardest and most fundamental responsibility that you will take on is facing your codependency and that of the people who are closest to you. You will be taking a huge leap of faith so you can become vulnerable with the hopes of being a person who is more confident in the future. For this transformation to happen, you have to learn how to walk through your world with grace and confidence, set the right boundaries for you, interact with people in a direct but kind manner, and be assertive when dealing with problems.

Learning to Be a Better Member of Your Family

After you learned your codependency patterns went back to the family, you might have discovered some skeletons within that closet. If you have denied any abuse or shortcomings within your family, this might have been a painful revelation. You have to explore your family's origins in order to understand your codependency. Remember that you aren't perfect, so this means that your family isn't going to be perfect.

Family Origins

You need to use your journal and think about your family. Try to write down any behaviors or patterns that could have caused your codependency. Create a heading for all members of your family and try to answer the following questions:

- What feelings did you feel the most when being around this person?

- From the things you know now, are they codependent?

- Was this person around when you needed them?

- From the things you know now, are they narcissistic?

- Did this person express feelings easily?

- Were they chronically mentally or physically ill?

- Did they blow up or yell when they got angry?

- Has this person broken any laws or engaged in dangerous or reckless activities?

- Did this person push any mistaken beliefs onto you?

- Did this person ever get addicted to spending, anger, smoking, gambling, alcohol, drugs, etc.?

- Did this person ever model any codependent behaviors for you? What were they?

- How did they deal with anger and handle conflicts?

- Did they make you feel loved?

- Were they ever sexually, emotionally, or physically abusive?

After you have written about all your family members and used these questions, see if you can affirm or find out what you know about your family and how they might have unknowingly planted the seeds of your codependency.

Now, take the time to look back on what you have discovered and see if there are unresolved issues within your family. It doesn't help to dig up hurt and pain and leave it unattended.

Figure out if you can resolve these issues by yourself or if you need to address them with a specific member of your family. Your goal is to stop being the victim. What can you do to stop these ghosts from bothering you now?

There are a few ways you can look at the information you found out about your family. One way is to find out how these things are affecting your current relationships, how they might change your behavior with them. The second way is to figure out if you should confront the issues you have with specific family members. Will this help to lessen the power they have over you?

Some people like to work with just their current family members, meaning children and partner. Some want to talk to their parents and family members that were around when they were growing up. It all depends on the person and how much they have dug into the past. They might have found some skeletons they need to deal with.

Finding Skeletons

One of my clients, Charlene, remembered that she was abused by her older sister when she was a child through writing in her journal, mindfulness, and reading. Her sister was constantly jumping out and scaring her. She would lock her in her bedroom, turn the lights out, steal her belongings, break her toys, beat her up, choke her, and smother her. Charlene told others and herself that she had a good childhood except for a bit of "sibling rivalry."

After Charlene decided to take a closer look at her childhood, she experienced the pain again. She realized that it was necessary to look at the relationship she had with her sister. She also wondered about her parents. Where were her parents? Why weren't they around to protect her? Why didn't Charlene tell her parents, stop the abuse, or do anything? Charlene decided to see a therapist to get help for her anxiety and depression that was triggered by these memories.

With therapy, Charlene realized that she really didn't trust people. Because she didn't truly trust her husband, it made her suspicious and controlling. This caused unfounded accusations and arguments that got explosive. She also realized that most of the time she still felt like a victim. She constantly braced herself, waiting for someone to hurt her. Charlene decided to talk to her husband about this and asked for his help with the childhood abuse triggers. Charlene was able to work on her issues with trust with help from her husband. This, in turn, helped their relationship.

Charlene hadn't contacted her sister for a long time and really expected not to ever see her again. She didn't want to confront her about all the abuse. She decided to write to her sister a letter in her journal. She didn't plan on sending it to her. During her therapy, her sister got sick and asked Charlene if she could come for a visit. Charlene began to panic. She talked about her feelings and thoughts with the therapist.

Charlene decided it was time to talk with her parents and tell them what she experienced while growing up. She told them about being afraid each day. She finally asked them why they never stepped in and tried to stop the abuse. Her parents seemed shocked by the news. They profusely apologized and asked if there were anything they could do now to help her. Charlene decided to forgive them. This alliance with her parents made Charlene feel better about facing her sister. Charlene didn't feel like she was a victim of all of them. She felt affirmed since her parents understood and could help her be nice to her sister.

Charlene chose to deal with the origin of her issues where she felt the most pain. She devoted a lot of therapy time working through childhood abuse and this helped her talk with her parents. She felt like she had resolved the issues with her parents and decided she wouldn't confront her sister.

There will never be a wrong or right decision when talking about family origin wounds. If they are still being abusive, you might decide to tell them to stop. You might decide to stop spending time with them and put firm boundaries into place. You might even decide to deal with each unwanted behavior as they come up. It is completely up to you.

Learning to Be a Better Friend

When you start changing and moving toward a life without codependency, you are going to attract new friends. These friendships will be more interdependent and mutual. While working toward being an equal friend, you will have two different aspects of friendship to write about in your journal.

Who Are Your Friends?

Just like you wrote in your journal about your family, you are going to do the same thing with your friends. Don't worry about acquaintances, just people whom you consider your real friends. Write all their names at the top of the page. If you only have a few close friends, that is fairly normal. You might want to include friends that you consider your second-tier friends. Now you have to decide if old friends still fit with the new you. If these friendships are codependent, you can decide to move on, or you might decide to work on moving the friendship into a better place.

Answer each of these questions to help you decide:

- Are your friends too demanding?

- Are your friends always seeking your advice?

- Is your friend fragile or unstable?

- Are your friends not interested in what you are going through and don't realize you are struggling?

- Do your friends call often and expect you to stop and talk with them?

- Do you have to walk on eggshells when you are around them?

- When talking with your friend, do they talk more than 50 percent of the time?

- Do your friends cancel lunch dates or just not show up?

- If you aren't available, does your friend get mad?

You might realize that some friends aren't enhancing your life. You are the only person who will know if the friendship is hopeless and you should move on. If you do decide to try and help them, these friendships might be helpful in giving you opportunities to constantly work on your codependency. Let's see what Mark did with his friends:

Mark Looks at His Friends

Mark has three close friends. Frank is his roommate. They work in the same place and see each other every day, but they don't have deep discussions. They ride to work together, and their involvement is based on the apartment they share. Mark looks at his friendship with Frank and realizes it is interdependent and they don't need to work on it.

Mark has another friend whom he met at work. David works in a different department than Mark, but they are compatible. They have worked together on many projects and had great results. They eat lunch together often. They usually talk about their work, hobbies, and video games. David talks a bit more than Mark, but he likes getting Mark's opinion on things. If Mark were more withdrawn, he might be more of a listener and find himself in the role of a therapist. He enjoys talking with David. Their friendship is an equal one.

According to his journal entries, Mark's third friend is the problem. Carl also works at the same place but is needy and depends on Mark to help him on all his projects. Lately, he has been asking for favors that don't have to do with work. He is single, and Mark is drawn to him because Carl needs Mark to help him. At first, Mark is pleased that Carl asked him and enjoys Carl's reliance and gratitude. Helping Carl makes Mark feel good. After Mark has worked on his codependency, he realizes that Carl's friendship isn't healthy. Mark has set boundaries by telling Carl that he is willing to help out at work, but he doesn't have time to help after hours.

Mark was able to use journaling to spot problem areas in his friendships. This helped him see where he needed to set boundaries and with whom. This is just one way that journaling can help you to improve your codependency. This was the first big change I started to make in healing my codependency when I noticed my problem.

Resolving Problems with Friends

Examine your friends by writing in your journal. Are there any unresolved problems that you have been afraid to talk with them about? Create a list for all your friends and process each one. You need to decide if you can get rid of problems you can't control or if you just don't want to deal with them. If problems are still there, try to approach them. If you can learn to be more forthright and honest with your friends and they become offensive, you now have new information that can help you make better decisions about your friendship.

Before you begin talking with your friend, you need to know what you want to achieve. What is motivating you? If you are motivated to strengthen the friendship and resolve things by being honest, go ahead. If you feel brave enough to let them know they are a jerk, just save your breath and let them go.

Evaluate New Friends

While you are changing, new people are going to come into your life. They will see you as compassionate, well-adjusted, and assertive, a person who can be honest about what they are feeling and is direct about their boundaries and expectations. That might not be what they are looking for. They might want to fulfill some of their codependency needs. They might want a codependent friend who will take care of them.

You have learned enough about codependency to see red flags in friendships and relationships. Take care of any concerns you have immediately. Remember that you can put yourself and your needs first and stop a friendship that isn't healthy at any time. If a new friend starts canceling all get-togethers at the beginning of the friendship, this might indicate that they really aren't interested in you. This shows that they think their needs are more important than your own. If new friends begin asking for favors, this could show they are very needy. If a new friend constantly talks about themselves, that isn't good. If a new friend gets offended easily, gossips about other friends, is moody, misunderstands you a lot, all of these are red flags.

There is an old saying that goes, "Partners come and go, but friends are forever."

Yes, friends are important for our emotional well-being, and some friendships do last a lifetime. Just make sure you pick your friends wisely.

Learning to Be a Better Worker

Once you start evaluating new friends, you might start noticing that codependency doesn't just show up in your personal relationships; it can appear in your working relationships as well. After all, you and your coworkers naturally depend on each other already as you work towards a common goal, try to keep a business going, and attempt to survive customers or clients together. If you have a codependent personality, you could be tempted—compelled, even—to go overboard as you attempt to earn the approval of your coworkers, management, and/or boss. But just like codependency in personal relationships, it can be worked through—once you recognize and acknowledge that it is happening.

Identifying Codependency at Work

Codependents are not easy to identify in the workplace. After all, codependents are often good employees, working harder than everyone else as they try to live up to their own perfectionist standards. Still, it's not impossible. Whether they're bosses or just coworkers, there are a few tell-tale signs that give away workplace codependents. These can include inexplicable or hair-trigger anger, excessive stress, micromanagement, overstepping boundaries on a project, etc.

If you think that you might be a workplace codependent, ask yourself the following questions:

- When you started the job, were you overly nice to both your coworkers and your boss? While not solely a trait of codependents, codependents do tend to at least start out at their job being overly nice to everyone to ensure that they have everyone's approval, not just their boss'.

- Do you take on far more work and hours than you really should? This can be brushed off as just needing the extra hours to cover the rent, but workplace codependents also accept as much work as possible and volunteer to work longer hours in order to make people think they are helpful and like them.

- Do you offer unsolicited advice to your coworkers, even on matters that don't have to do with your job or work at all? Like I said in "Signs of Codependency", codependents like to offer advice even when they haven't been asked and will push it to be followed, and it's no different at work. No different, that is, except that the boundary is pushed even further since the advice could easily overstep what is acceptable for the relationship between coworkers.

- Do you micromanage everything? Since codependents are perfectionists, everything must be just right for them or else they'll feel like failures. At work, they will not delegate unless they are absolutely forced to, and even then, they'll hover over the other person's shoulder relentlessly. If you're in a management position, this could go into overdrive and cause you to all but take complete control of the project. Some codependents will do this to projects and tasks that aren't even theirs.

- Do you need constant approval and recognition or else you worry that you did something wrong or start to feel unappreciated? Just like codependent needs to be acknowledged all the time for everything that they do in a personal relationship, a workplace codependent also needs it there. Otherwise, they'll either obsessively fret over the thought that they did something wrong/someone doesn't like them or they'll get mad from feeling unappreciated.

- Have you been getting easily frustrated, stressed, and angry at work, especially towards your coworkers and boss? This could just be the normal kind of emotional turmoil that everyone experiences when they feel overwhelmed by their job. However, codependents will experience these emotions if they start to feel unappreciated, as though their hard work isn't being reciprocated, and/or that their advice is being ignored.

- Have you sacrificed your personal life for your work? Codependency can sometimes be the source of workaholism. Codependents give up everything else, especially those things related to their own care, in order to make sure that everything/everyone at work is taken care of.

There is a fine line between the signs of a great employee and the signs of a codependent employee. Sometimes, a boss might just ignore the bad signs so long as the good ones continue to benefit the business. So, it's up to you to look out for yourself. If you notice yourself answering "yes" to any of the above questions, stop and work to improve it like you are in your personal relationships.

And if you notice a coworker showing similar symptoms, feel free to suggest the possibility of codependency to them and even offer them this book or some other resources. Just remember that you must take care of yourself first, and that is all you are responsible for.

The Importance of Reducing Codependency at Work

Every relationship in your life will improve when you improve your codependent behavior. However, there is incredible urgency behind reigning in your codependent behavior in the workplace, and not all of the reasons have to do with your job itself.

The most prominent reason is that, after some time, your work will suffer. You will be overworked, but you probably will resist telling anyone because you will just want to make sure that everyone else at work is taken care of first. You will be drained as you take on more and more work to ingratiate yourself to everyone, and as the stress you put on yourself to take care of everyone and everything grows, your work ethic and the quality of your work will reduce drastically.

All of your relationships will suffer, including those at work. As time goes on, the codependent relationship will demand more of your time. The resulting workaholism will edge out every other part of your life: hobbies, fun nights out, and even loved ones. You'll work right through girl's/boy's night out, leave early to pick up coffee for the office instead of spending some time with your child before school, you're too tired after running yourself ragged at work and sleep right through date night, and so on. Just remember: the sooner you get your codependency at work under control, the sooner the rest of your life will start to balance.

Your relationships with your coworkers and/or boss will also begin to suffer for any number of reasons. While you might think of yourself as helpful and hardworking when you offer to do all these tasks outside of your normal scope, others might see it as overreaching or, if you are in a management position, micromanaging. Similarly, unsolicited advice might wear your coworkers' patience thin, and if offer it to your boss/management and insist they take it—just feel lucky if you still have a job after that. Even a constant need for approval and praise can irritate other people, and when you start to feel underappreciated because you don't get it, the resulting anger, frustration, and irritability will only tear your relationships down more quickly.

Inversely, your coworkers or boss could take you up on your offers a little *too* often. They start to pile more and more work on you, ask you to help with or even take over extra tasks, or come seeking your advice on projects that are not in your department and are probably way out of your field of expertise. You might even end up like Mark in our earlier example with your own Carl (or maybe more): a coworker who comes to you for advice on and help with matters outside of work. Maybe some of them, like your Carl, will show gratitude and reliance, and you will appreciate that—no, crave it. Others, though, will not even give it a second thought. When they don't, you will, again, start to feel underappreciated and have that anger and bitterness boil to the surface, eventually eroding at the bonds of what could have been a good working relationship.

Finally—but most importantly—is your own health. Allowing yourself to be a codependent worker, as is the case with being a codependent in any relationship, causes you to neglect yourself. I don't just mean that you will not eat right or that you might forget to go to the doctor, get the flu shot, or forget to shower (although those could certainly come up if you let work take over your life). No, it can also affect your health in many, many invisible ways. In fact, your mental and emotional health will not only be neglected because all of your attention is on work and your coworkers; your codependency could directly add to the strain it's already under.

Research suggests that your workplace environment can directly affect your mental and emotional health. For example, a 2010 study from Sweden concluded that being the victim of workplace bullying can cause an increase in your anxiety and stress levels.[2] The turmoil that is stress and anxiety rarely come alone, also. Every part of our bodies is so intricately connected that if something is thrown out of balance in our minds and/or our emotions, something in our physical bodies will most likely be thrown off as well. According to an article in *Business Insider* by Patricia Thompson called "How your job can impact your health – and your weight", even normal spikes in this kind of workplace stress, such as a horrible boss, can then have adverse effects on your health: raise your blood pressure, lead to heart disease and obesity, disrupt your sleep patterns, etc.

The more you overwork yourself trying to ingratiate yourself to your boss and/or coworkers, the more underappreciated you feel, the angrier and more frustrated you get from feeling underappreciated, the more your anxiety and stress will grow. The higher your anxiety and stress levels, the faster your health will deteriorate. In the end, it isn't just a matter of improving your codependence at work for psychological reasons; it's for your very health.

Take a look at the case of one of my more recent clients, Susan B.

Susan B. has just begun to take the first steps to overcoming her codependency in her personal relationships, especially with her long-time boyfriend. She has already realized through journaling that she and her parents had a codependent relationship when she was a child, in which she always tried to be the "son her father never had" by cleaning up the garage and helping him work on the car whenever he asked without fail and stayed "Mommy's little Einstein" by keeping up perfect grades, even when the doctor told her the stress had given her an ulcer as a high school senior. She has also been working on setting boundaries with her boyfriend and telling herself that he won't think she's selfish for taking some time for herself.

After she had to reschedule her appointments for a couple of weeks, she came into my office and explained to me that she had been in the hospital briefly and on bedrest. When I asked her what happened, she told me this story:

Susan B. started a new job about four months ago at a tech company. She wanted badly to get the approval of all of her coworkers, who had many more years of experience than she did, and particularly her new boss. Right from the start, she went out of her way to get in everyone's good graces. She left for work early to buy everyone on her team coffee, picked up lunch orders, stayed late to finish work ahead of their deadlines, and jumped at every chance she could get to offer her teammates advice before they even needed help. They nicknamed her "Our Psychic Angel" for her kindness and ability to predict just what they needed.

Three months into this routine, and Susan B. noticed that her coworkers were not been praising her as much as they used to. She worried that she wasn't working as hard as she should or that they didn't think she did a good job anymore, so she put in even more hours to keep everyone's favor. She missed her sister's birthday party to stay at work and finish a project three days early. She got up even earlier to get the coffee *and* arrive before her teammates to get a head start. When none of this seemed to get more than a one-time "That's great!" from her boss and team leader, Susan B. started to feel underappreciated and grew furious. She had done so much for them the past three months, and that was all she got? Didn't she get more than a couple people telling her "That's great"? Even as she stewed in her fury, she started to obsessively worry over her work and work ethic. Did she mess up on the last project? Did she finish something late and not realize it? Did she do something wrong? Did none of her coworkers like her anymore? She even considered sending out her resume to get a fresh start somewhere she'd be appreciated.

Then one day, all of this stress came to a head when her team leader pulled her aside to talk to her about some code that she had programmed that needed to be fixed. In the face of this presumed criticism, Susan B. started to fill with dread and concern that she was not liked in the office and that her work was no good. Her stress and anxiety spiked, and so did her blood pressure. She started to experience chest pains, and while she tried to hide it, her team leader noticed and called her an ambulance. It was a good thing he did, because by the time they got to the hospital, it was determined that she was having a minor heart attack.

Susan B. has told me from the beginning that she has had high blood pressure from stress that started when she overextended herself as a high senior just to keep her mother happy. Now, as an adult, she has done the same again, only with her coworkers, team leader, and boss—and it might have all been avoided.

Even though Susan B. knew that she had code-pendency issues in her personal life, she didn't see it in her work life. When it didn't result in the continuous praise and gratitude that she needed, it started to make her angry, which made her stressed, and she started to take on more work, which made her even more stressed. In the end, Susan B.'s codependency at work put her health at risk. However, such an incident can be prevented if workplace codependency is handled as persistently as codependency in personal relationships is.

Be Your Own Advocate

Once you recognize and realize that you need to improve on codependency in the workplace, you might still hesitate to act. Work is a much more public place than among friends, family, or other loved ones, even among neighbors. Being able to explain what's going on, let alone be understood and have your wishes respected, can feel almost impossible on your own there. Even if you had just one other person to give you some support, you might not have such a hard time at it.

The sad truth is that there is no guarantee that anyone else at work is going to look out for you at work. You're all there for one reason and one reason only: to work. Unless the quality of your work or your productivity starts to decline, odds are that most coworkers and especially your boss or management won't notice that something is wrong, let alone bother to ask you about it. There might be some kind soul who will try to talk to you when you start getting snappy and frustrated at being underappreciated, but you cannot rely on such kindness to appear, let alone try to stand up for you in front of those who might want to take advantage of your codependency.

Addressing codependency at work is not much different from what you will be doing to improve it in all the other areas of your life. However, there are two areas in particular that will be even harder to apply at work than everywhere else: setting boundaries and assertiveness.

You are probably struggling to do things like setting boundaries with friends and other loved ones in codependent relationships, so why would it be any different learning to say "no" to people who help decide—directly or indirectly—if you're going to continue getting paid through that company?

This feeling doesn't get any better when you're constantly reminded that we have to "keep our noses to the grind" to succeed in life or that we just need to "pull ourselves up by our bootstrap" in order to "climb the social/corporate ladder". A different kind of anxiety might take place of the anxiety over someone likes you or not. Here's what you need to keep in mind about this mentality: you can't very well climb the corporate ladder if you are weighed down by everyone else's weight.

Just like you wrote in your journal about your family and your friends, it's now time to do the same about your coworkers, management, and boss. This time, though, it won't be to decide whom to cut out and whom to keep. After all, you can't always choose whom you work with, and you usually can't walk away from a job lightly. Instead, you are going to think about which boundaries you specifically need to make for each person you work with, which ones you need to be more assertive with, and which of your coworkers you need to be more careful around. It might be a lot to remember and try to take into account in the moment, but after some practice, it will come more naturally and will save you a lot of problems in the long run.

While doing this exercise, remember to consider only those with whom you work directly and re-member to add more people as you change shifts or other people are shuffled around. If you get a new job, make sure to put at least one blank page in between these entries so that you will not get the two confused.

Now, at the top of the page, list their names and positions (simplify it to coworker, management, boss, or owner so that things won't get too messy or perplexing). Along the left-hand side of the page, write the following questions:

- Do they guilt or flatter me into doing stuff for them?

- Do they ask me to pick up extra work a lot?

- Do they try to push work on me even if I don't know how to do some of it?

- Do they try to ask me for a lot of work-related favors?

- Do they ask me for advice even if it's outside of the scope of my job and/or isn't something I would know about?

- Do they ask me to stay late a lot?

- Do they ask me to come in early a lot?

- Do they try to get me to give them advice on stuff outside of work even if it's not something I would know anything about?

- Do they try to ask favors of me outside of work?

- Do they call me at all hours, even if my job has set office hours and not shifts?

After you write out these questions, go through them for each person you work with and mark down if the answer is a "Yes", "No", or "Sometimes". For those which you have answered "Yes" or "Sometimes", you will want to make a rule for yourself to set up a boundary when it comes to this person and this particular issue. If it helps, make a list for each person that contains each action that will be considered off-limits—or at least limited—for them. If you find that someone has been answered as "Yes" or "Sometimes" for many or all of these questions, you will want to make a note to be careful with this person. They might be codependent, or they might be taking advantage of you. Either way, you'll want to proceed with caution. In some cases, you might even want to avoid them as much as possible, requesting shifts that they don't work if you can.

Codependency and Your Boss

After her first visit following her heart attack, I had Susan B. carry out the exercise I have outlined in the section above. Once she was done filling out the chart, she noticed that three of her coworkers in particular kept coming up at "Yes" or "Sometimes", one of them receiving one of those answers for every single question: two of her teammates, Laura and Ben, and her team leader, Sam.

With Laura and Ben, Susan B. realized that they were asking a lot of her outside of work. Laura kept asking her to do things like look into vintage video games and consoles because of Susan B.'s connections with some collectors. Ben, on the other hand, called her at all hours, always taking up more than half of the conversation talking about himself and then asking her advice on very personal matters. Susan B. had always tried to accommodate them because she wanted them to like her, but after looking at the chart, she knew that she had to set some boundaries with them and let them know that she could only help them with work-related matters, nothing else.

When it came to Sam, Susan B. wasn't sure what to do. Thinking back, she could see that most of the increased stress she had experienced leading up to her heart attack had come from taking on a lot of extra tasks for Sam, sometimes staying at the office until well after 10 o'clock at night and then getting in by 7 o'clock the next morning. She had even begun to learn a new programming language to help him with one project, but she hated trying to learn something she was so unfamiliar with and it had made her anxiety worse.

When I told her that that must have caused her blood pressure to raise and trigger her heart attack, Susan B. didn't disagree with me, but she told me that she didn't know what to do about it. Sam was the team leader. If he wanted her to work late on a project, she would work late on a project. If he wanted her to work early, she would work early. Learn a new program, take on far too many tasks without complaining, she would do anything short of something that would involve him directly harming her if it meant that he thought she was competent and worth keeping around. She's thirty-five years old and even at her age still has student loans to pay off, what is she supposed to do?

"Boundaries will work with my coworkers because they don't sign my paychecks," Susan B. explained to me.

It made sense, of course. What should you do when you have become a codependent at work and now your boss is all but demanding that the behavior continue? Do you set boundaries? Assert them? Try to find some middle ground? Or fold and just hope that being codependent in one area of your life won't influence you to let it happen again in other areas?

It's one thing to set up boundaries with a coworker, but a team leader or management? The *boss*? That might be a bit trickier. After all, if they want you to work later, it's not going to necessarily look good if you tell them "no". The same goes for if they ask you for advice or tell you to complete a task; you don't want to risk them thinking that you're incompetent, inexperienced, or too ignorant for your job, even if they're asking about something that isn't a part of your job description. That's just normal fear of losing your job, right?

The truth is that most bosses probably won't care too much. If you say that you can't work overtime, they'll just get someone else to do it. If you tell them that you can't give advice on something because it's outside of your field of expertise and it's not part of your job description, they'll understand and go ask someone else. If you tell them that you can't complete a task because you don't know how to do it, they'll either show you how to do it, have someone show you how to do it, or get someone else to do it. They won't think any less of you or, frankly, think twice about it at all. They are just there to get their work done. They won't judge you for not overachieving all day, every day, or for not bending over backwards for them when you don't know how.

If they do have a problem with it, you might have another problem on your hands altogether. It could be something as simple as a controlling boss. Perhaps they're just arrogant. They might even be narcissistic and abuse all of their employees through these kinds of insults and unrealistic expectations, especially if they're dealing with something that they're being forced to admit that they cannot do, thus cracking their perfect image of themselves.

However, there could be another side to the controlling aspect: your boss could be a codependent as well. The easiest way to tell is to just watch your boss for a while and see if you can notice any of the signs I talked about near the beginning of this book. Still, you can't be there to observe your boss all day, every day, so there are a few signs that could be more easily noticed in codependent bosses in particular:

- Perfectionism

    This one might seem like a given for any boss, but this is especially true for bosses who are codependent. They will accept nothing less than perfect and may the Lord help you if it is not right the first time. You can find this perfectionism in how they micromanage or even take on more tasks than they can handle rather than divide them among their workers.

- Off-the-Charts Stress Levels

    All bosses are going to be pretty stressed. We know that. Employees can be unruly, and we know that customers definitely can be, too. Nevertheless, the codependent bosses' need to be liked and tremendous perfectionism will force them to be on edge all the time. They could explode at the drop of a hat, especially if something goes wrong. To them, any problem would reflect back on them, and people might start to dislike them or see them as flawed.

- Simultaneously Overly Friendly and Overly Critical

  A codependent boss wants—*needs*—you to like them, for everyone to like them. At the same time, they will also trash talk you, especially if they feel at any point that they are underappreciated for their work. They will also be overly critical of you if it will deflect any blame off of them for a mistake they made or problem resulting from their actions so that everyone will still like and appreciate them and what they do.

- They Are Their Own Harshest Critics

  Like all codependents, they are their own worst critics, and this shows up in how they lead others. They cannot err, and therefore, their workers cannot err. If they fail at all, they will dive more into their workaholic behavior in order to ensure that they do not err again.

156

If you realize that your boss is a codependent, you will have to proceed with extra caution to avoid entering the same sort of codependent relationships you've had in your personal life. Unfortunately, they might also be the ones that will give you the hardest time in setting up these boundaries. They will want to micromanage your time for the job, and so they might get furious if you were not available for more hours if you assert yourself and decline to come in earlier or stay later. They will expect your work to be perfect, triggering your own insecurities. In the end, the work environment could be very unproductive for both you and your codependent boss.

Whether your boss is also a codependent or not, if you find that you cannot get your boss to respect your boundaries and asserting yourself is not making a difference, you might be facing a very tough decision. At the end of the day, it's about doing what's best for you. If you cannot fix your workplace environment to improve your freedom from codependence, you might have to cut it loose and look for another job.

Improving Your Freedom from Being Codependent

Every single person you meet during your life and all the situations you face give you an opportunity to fine-tune your freedom from being codependent. How can change happen, and what can you do to help it along? Every year research discovers something new about human behavior. Psychiatrists used to believe that personality disorders can't be changed. Now the opposite holds true. What people believe about the influences on human behavior has always swung like a pendulum. It was first thought that it was just a brain thing. Then it turned into an environment/brain thing. Now, due to the advances in neurotechnology, research has a new excitement about the human brain. Many believe the world of neuropsychology is going to continuously evolve.

Those changes you have been trying so hard to reach are extremely possible to achieve. Your main goal is to nourish and develop your identity. Yes, you have an identity. You are just trying to remold it. Codependency traits are continuous.

You could be more or less codependent. You might show one or fifty codependency traits.

You have been given new awareness, insights, and tools that will help you fix your self-esteem, be more confident, and increase your sense of self. You will constantly be working on your transformation by watching your behaviors, thoughts, and feelings. You make any and all adjustments as you go along. You have to be present in your relationships, love and value yourself, and find your voice. You have to love yourself with all your flaws. You might find that you have all kinds of power to expand your happiness.

Chapter 10: Removing Codependent Communication

If you were to record a fight between yourself and your spouse, you might realize that codependency reared its ugly head during the argument. You need to develop a vocabulary and communication skills that will move you from codependency to interdependency. It is similar to learning how to speak a new language. You didn't learn these skills while in school, and it isn't likely you learned anything from your friends or family. You need to take responsibility for the way you communicate. You need to build a bridge that leads away from your true self while pursuing true connections with others.

Focus on "I"

One crucial part of communicating well is using "I" messages. This tool has been a part of the training for United States diplomats that was created 50 years ago by the government. This message is outlined on the United States Department of State's website. Now, the "I" message is a skill that is learned during couple's therapy. You are also going to learn how to use this tool.

- Internal Shift

When you use an "I" message, it restructures the way you think and makes you self-reflect before speaking. Because language shapes our reality, each time you use "I" rather than "YOU" when trying to resolve conflicts, you are changing your internal reality. This forces you to identify and process the way you feel and the way you perceive things before your mouth even opens to talk about the problem. Just think about how automatic and easy it is to begin an argument with "You constantly do..." What does this type of language show you? You are viewing yourself as a victim. You want the other person to be at fault and apologize to you.

- External Shift

During couple's therapy, a therapist will start the communication training by introducing the "I" message. It focuses on the external or, basically, what an "I" message is and how you can use it to start a conversation and help resolve conflicts.

This is part of the behavioral intervention. Most of the time, it would be better to begin with changing your behavior and working toward an emotional and cognitive shift that will follow.

When you begin couple's therapy, the whole purpose behind it is for both you and your partner to change. You are responsible for changing you. Your partner is responsible for changing themselves. Many couples start therapy already willing to begin firing at their partner. In order to get ready for the next session, take time to think about ways you might contribute to the problems you have in the relationship.

How many times has a discussion started with "You never", "You need to", or "You always"? When you use "You" statements, it means you are putting the blame on your partner for the things you are experiencing. You are painting a picture that you are the victim and are making your partner explain or defend themselves. It is hard to think that starting a discussion with "I" could have a large influence on the way a conversation will proceed, but it can and will work. It is as challenging and as simple as that. Just change the word "you" for the word "I" when you begin a sentence and watch the change.

"I" Formula

The "I" message is made up of three components: the way you feel, what caused you to feel this way, and the reasons why you have these feelings. It looks a bit like this: "I feel (a feeling, not a thought) when you (a non-judgmental description of behavior) because (a reason why you feel how you feel)". It might look like this if you filled in the blanks: "I feel threatened when you scream at me to turn off the radio since music helps relax me."

Here are a few examples of "I" messages that you could use when trying to resolve a conflict:

- "I feel frustrated when your answer is defensive because this makes me think we can't talk to each other anymore and are getting further apart."

- "I feel sad when you won't talk to me because my parents wouldn't talk to me when I was younger, which made me feel alone."

- "I feel hopeless when you have promised time and time again that you will stop drinking and I see empty beer bottles in the trash because this makes me think you are either an alcoholic or becoming one and won't admit it and you will never get any better."

- "I feel angry when you tell me I'm lazy because I'm not. I do things my way and in my time."

- "I feel rejected when you laugh and make fun of me because my mom always made fun of me and it hurt."

These examples show that when you give an "I" message, it requires you to examine your feelings and the reasons behind them. It makes you share these with your significant other without blaming them. Look at this statement and compare it with the previous one to see if you can figure out why it isn't a good "I" statement. See how it gets corrected until it fits into the correct formula.

1. "I feel you aren't listening to me because you are watching that stupid car show because you are a selfish jerk and this is all you ever care about."

2. "I feel unimportant* because you are watching that stupid car show because you are a selfish jerk and this is all you ever care about."

3. "I feel unimportant* because you won't look at me when I talk* because you are a selfish jerk and cars are all you ever think about."

4. "I feel unimportant because you won't look at me when I talk because I need direct eye contact so I can feel like you are listening to me."

When resolving conflicts, using the pronoun "I" shows you are willing to share yourself. When you use the pronoun "you", it shows you are blaming others. If communication could be shown by using arrows, arrows would point to the speaker with the speaker's "I" message. In contrast, an arrow would point to another person when you use a "you" statement. "You" statement arrows could be deflected by the recipient and any resolution might end then and there with just a few words being spoken.

Resolving Conflicts – To Whom Does the Problem Belong?

Most couples get along fine until it's time to re- solve their problems. It isn't reasonable to think that both parties might see the problem in the same way. The conflict isn't the enemy, like many want to believe. Any normal relationship is going to have conflicts. When couples avoid the conflict or argue until they are tired of arguing, the con- flict turns into a monster that lurks in the shad- ows. It is ready to jump out at the first oppor- tunity.

The great part of good communication is that every person respects and values the other per- son's opinion and it doesn't matter how different they are. They accept the other person's right to feel and think the way they do and, thus, starts the beginning of a compromise. Here's an example from one of my couple's therapy sessions:

Frank hates it when Grace leaves her beauty products all over the bathroom vanity. He has asked her numerous times to put the stuff away when she gets through with it. Every time she explains why she didn't: she forgot, she was in a hurry, she can get out the door faster if she doesn't put it up, there isn't room for her to put it away, etc. She promised time and again that she will start being more aware but every day the products stay on the vanity.

Each time Frank finds her stuff on the vanity, he fumes a bit more inside. He gives up on trying to change his wife, but every time they disagree on something, he always brings up how inconsiderate she is when she doesn't put her products away because she knows it bothers him so much.

So, the question is who owns the problem? Some might say it is Grace's since she won't put her things away. If Grace's husband didn't care that she left her things on the counter, they wouldn't have a problem, would they?

Has there ever been a part of your life where you have always gotten everything you needed, wanted, or expected? No. Most people believe this is still possible with marriage. It is better to accept the fact that you might get the things you want the majority of the time and the rest has to be negotiated. Try to develop ways to negotiate and learn how to compromise.

When couples go to therapy, the first thing each one says is it is the other person's fault. It makes sense if the husband states a problem that he is actually the one with the problem. The therapist already knows this, but they need to teach it to their clients. If you were to ask Frank, he would say the problem is Grace's. Grace might even agree with him if she is codependent.

If you don't know with whom or where to begin, how in the world will you ever resolve a conflict? It would be like trying to play football if you can't figure out who is kicking off. When you have figured it out, it would then be possible to get down the field. Frank kicks off with the problem of the vanity.

Take Responsibility for Feelings

Learning to communicate in a way that encourages people to take responsibility for their feelings is a way to help with resolving conflicts. When looking at Frank and Grace's therapy session, it starts with Frank stating he has a problem. He took responsibility for the problem and the way he feels about it. He will then use "I" messages to convey his feelings to Grace. When she has accurately received the message, Frank will give Grace three options for ways she can help him with the problem. Grace will then willingly agree to one, two, or all the options. She might also decide to not agree.

The session will get rid of the big obstacles that usually happen when the couple tries to fix a conflict. The therapist will intentionally ask them to give an actual conflict so they can start slowly, but they will quickly feel what successful resolution will feel like. These tools will work on complicated conflicts, and they work each time. With time, they will become effortless for Grace and Frank and melt all the animosity that has accumulated over the years from frustration. Conflicts will happen when you are in a relationship, so learning how to move through them smoothly and constantly will enforce new behaviors. All couples should be invested in communicating well with each other since there will be an immediate pay-off for them both.

Here is an example session:

Therapist: "Frank, you have a problem with the vanity. Would you like to begin with an 'I' message?"

Frank turns toward Grace and with the help of the therapist: "I feel hurt and dismissed when you leave products all over the vanity because I can be a bit of a neat freak and it causes my anxiety to take over when I have to deal with all that clutter every morning."

Therapist: "Grace, don't explain or defend yourself. Just say back what you heard Frank say."

Grace turns toward Frank with the help of the therapist: "You feel hurt when I leave my products on the vanity because it makes you feel anxious."

Therapist: "Frank, is this correct?"

Frank: "Pretty much, I feel dismissed, too, like, I don't matter or I'm not important. I guess I also want Grace to acknowledge that I did admit I am a bit obsessive."

Therapist: "Grace?"

Grace looks at Frank: "You feel hurt and unimportant when I leave all my products on the vanity. I noticed you said you were a bit of a neat freak. I do appreciate that."

Therapist: "Did she get the message, Frank?"

Frank: "Yes."

Therapist: "Now Frank, because this is your problem, would you like to ask Grace to help you?"

Frank smiles: "Yes."

Therapist: "I've told you that couples are not obligated to give each other anything, correct? If you would like to have a healthy relationship, both of you need to be willing to give to the other. If you don't, you aren't going to feel loved."

Quick Tip: When you were a child and misbehaved, your parent might have said something like: "Why did you do that?" Did they want you to tell them the reason for your actions or were they actually saying, "Don't do that"? Using the word, "Why" when trying to resolve a conflict can be a negative trigger from childhood on through adulthood. It will always cause the other party to go on the defensive. Try to use phrases such as "Help me understand," "I feel confused about this," or "I am not understanding what you mean."

• Choices

Therapist: "Frank, you are responsible for solving your own problem, but let's say you have a partner who loves you and who wants to help you with it. I want to ask Grace if she might think about giving you, as a gift, any of these three requests you will now make. Please make your request in this form: A, would you be willing to (state your first request); B, would you be willing to (give your second request); and C, would you be willing to (state your third request)."

Frank: "I don't need to ask for three things. I just want her to put her products away."

Therapist: "Well, Grace might agree to do that and that could be one of your requests. It will help to push you away from your one-dimensional position and move you to a compromise if you would be willing to think outside the box here and figure out some other options."

Frank, smiling, turns toward Grace: "Okay, Grace, would you be willing to put your things away?"

Therapist: "Great, that is request A. Now, what about B?"

Frank: "B, would you be willing to use the other bathroom on days I have early meetings?"

Therapist: "Now, C?"

Frank: "C, would you be willing to... (he turns toward the therapist) I can't think of a C."

Therapist: "Take some time to think outside the box."

Frank (pauses and thinks about it): "Okay, I think I have a C. C, there is that large drawer on the front of the vanity where we keep stuff for the bathroom. If we empty out that drawer, would you be willing to open the drawer and sweep all your products into it when you are done in the bathroom?"

Therapist: "Great. Grace, would you please repeat the requests back to Frank so he can make sure you heard his requests accurately. What was request A?"

Grace: "A, will I put my things away after I'm done with it; B, will I use the other bathroom when he has early meetings; C, we clean out the big drawer in the vanity and I just sweep my things into it when I get done."

Therapist: "Frank, did she get it right?"

Frank: "Pretty much, I guess it isn't reasonable to expect her to use the other bathroom."

Therapist: "You can ask for whatever you think will help. It is up to Grace to either agree or not agree. Now, Grace, you have the right to agree to one, two, or all the requests or you can choose to not agree to any of them. What do you think you would like to do?"

Grace: "To be honest, I don't want to move my things to the other bathroom. That was my least favorite request. I absolutely can't do B. I thought I could do A, but I have agreed to do that in the past and haven't done it yet. If we could empty that drawer, I could just do one huge sweep. I won't have to take time to put everything back in its own place. I can do that. I could do C. (She turns toward Frank) Are you sure you are willing to move all that stuff? Where will we put it?"

Therapist: "Frank is the one who suggested it, Grace. Why are you trying to talk him out of it when you have just reached an agreement? This could be your codependency surfacing. You aren't used to saying no to Frank. Are you feeling guilty?"

Grace shrugs her shoulders: "Probably, I don't want him to go to any trouble. I will do C."

Therapist: "Frank, is there anything you would like to say to Grace?"

Frank: "Not really."

Therapist: "She did just give you a gift."

Frank: "Fine. Thanks."

Therapist: "Very good, both of you. We have just used a cognitive behavioral technique to resolve Frank's problem with the vanity. You both have used new communication tools, which probably seem a bit hard right now. With some practice, you will begin to incorporate this into the way you talk and eventually it will become second nature."

Grace: "Do we have to remember all of this?"

Therapist: "That would be a lot to do in one sitting. No, I am going to give you a handout that you can take with you. It will let you practice using 'I' messages and this resolution exercise each day for 30 minutes. It will get easier with time."

Therapist: "We have begun at the behavioral level and I consider this problem solved. In summary, Frank, you agreed to clean the things out of the top drawer of the vanity. Will you be able to get it cleaned out today?"

Frank: "Yes."

Therapist: "That's great. Grace, beginning in the morning, you agreed to sweep your products into that drawer before you leave the bathroom. Correct?"

Grace: "Yes."

Therapist: "Every time you have a conflict, I'd like you to summarize the agreement just like I just did. Your goal is to be completely clear with each other. Tomorrow, you have an opportunity to put your plan to the test. We will be able to talk about it in our next session. Good job, you two."

Processing the Resolution Model

This looks fine on paper because it's a behavioral intervention. Empathy training, assertiveness training, communication training are all formulas that focus on behavior.

Quick Tip:

If you were to make a recording of the voices during a couple's therapy session, it might show that Line A shows 80 percent activity whereas Line B shows about 20 percent. This shows another communication problem and it is one that has been going on a long time. One partner will talk too much while, to others, one doesn't talk as much. Line A will talk more and become frustrated. Line B will stop listening and become frustrated.

When a therapist starts with new couples, the therapist will ask them to identify their problems. Communication is usually first on the list. If the couple can't talk to each other, they won't be able to solve their problems within their relationship. The most important role the therapist has is to figure out all the dysfunctional layers. It is extremely rare if couples know how to talk to each other when they start therapy. Communication training is the first thing that is done. If they try to prioritize therapy in any other way, it would be like pushing the couple into shark-infested waters.

After the couple can manage their conflicts, the new skills will become an umbrella that all other problems can be put under. Is therapy really that simple? Nope. Couple's therapy is very complex.

If it were easy, everyone would have it figured out. People seek out therapy because they have things that need to be fixed and they don't know how. One more role of the therapist is being a teacher.

Seeing the Struggle of Power

Most couples make a mistake by getting into a battle with each other when a problem arises. Each contestant will step on a platform where they will defend their truth. From their positions, each opponent will try every weapon in their arsenal to defeat their enemy, knock them off their platform while they remain steadfast in their own truths. The last person left standing is "right" and has won the battle.

Weapons Used to be Right

- "That is crazy, mean, silly, or ridiculous. You are upset about that?"

This weapon is called the "what is the matter with you". You are turning their concern back on them while discounting any possibility that the opponent could have true issues because they are flawed somehow. So, they are wrong, of course.

- "That isn't what I felt, did, or said and that isn't what you did or said."

This weapon is called rewriting history. It is used to prove the recollection of the opponent is false. They won't even know what actually happened and will always be wrong.

- "How can you say that?"

This will be accompanied by anger or tears. This weapon is called the "shut up, I can't handle this". You attack your opponent for some negative fault or for being insensitive. You emphasize they are wrong for trying to resolve the problem. The main goal is to make them feel bad so that they go away.

- "This is completely unfair. I would never get upset about something like this."

This weapon is called the "shame on you" or "the self-righteous". It is meant to stop their opponent by saying they are crazy for even having concerns. They are wrong for even feeling the way they do.

- "That totally pisses me off."

This weapon is called the "shut up or I will show you what anger truly is". It is designed to hurt the opponent if they don't back off.

- "I've seen you do that" or "You do the same thing"

This weapon is called "bound back". It is used to deflect your opponent's concerns back on them. It will deflate and divert their concerns by blaming them, and this discounts their rights to have their concern. This means they are wrong.

Did you see yourself in any of these arguments? Many people can identify with some of them because everyone wants to be right and it becomes a battle all too often.

These examples are very typical of a partner who is codependent and doesn't take into consideration a loved one's concern, remains centered in their own world, and doesn't want to listen. It will be impossible for them not to feel attacked over every little thing, and this causes them to defend themselves. Remember that a person who is codependent doesn't have an identity other than what they see in a mirror or what their partner thinks about them. Their only hope is to change the way their partner feels and thinks, tire them out, attack them, punish them, overpower them, or prove them wrong until they just give up.

Look back over the battle weapons and think about the skills you have been exposed to that could change the way you could use the weapons against your partner. These skills would be: being responsible for being unsatisfied, using "I" messages, and the three-option skill. You need to take time to think about how you can use these skills to prevent a battle.

Affirmation

This skill will set a tone for resolution and compromise. If your partner states a concern to you, the first thing for you to do is affirm. Many people will automatically get defensive. You need to affirm in a non-defensive way that you heard their concern. You do this by repeating what your partner has said in your own words.

Partner: "Why haven't you finished the laundry?"

You: "You thought I would have the laundry done by now?" (Be careful how you say this. The wrong tone of voice could start a fight. Make sure your tone stays neutral and non-confrontational.)

From this point, the tone has been established. "I have heard you, now let's talk about it." You have let the wind out of the angry sails and are showing you are somebody who is willing to listen to their concern and move on.

Affirmation isn't what you use at the start of a discussion. You use it completely through to get information from your partner and let them know you are there to help fix the problem. Here's an example:

Partner: "You were home all day, why didn't you get all the flowers planted?"

You: "You wanted it finished today before it started to rain tomorrow."

The first time you use this affirmation skill with your partner, they might look at you like you've gone completely crazy. Many people just wait for you to become defensive before they even get their complaint said. Most of the time, they are planning what they will say once you get defensive and angry.

Validation

Validation and affirmation are interchangeable. Each one will create a spirit of cooperation, and most of the time, they are used together. Validation can be used to accept the way your partner is feeling. If you were to add validation after affirmation, it might sound something like this:

You: "You thought I would have the flowers planted by now. I can totally understand why you would feel this way. It is dark now and it is supposed to rain tomorrow."

The validation sentence was the second sentence.

Here is how to add validation to another exchange:

Partner: "You were home all day, why couldn't you finish the planting? Now it's dark and it will rain tomorrow."

You: "You are thinking it is too dark now to plant. I know exactly what you mean, and I completely agree."

Even though this is important, if a couple can communicate, especially when there is a conflict, they don't use much affirmation or validation.

Quick Tip: Feelings aren't ever wrong. A thought or idea might be inaccurate or misguided and might need to be clarified. Try not to confuse feelings and thoughts by saying such things: "I feel you are just testing me." This is only a speculative thought. When the word "feel" gets used, you need to make sure you use an actual feeling such as tired, bored, calm, elated, happy, furious, confused, hurt, devastated, annoyed, irked, frustrated, sad, or mad.

You have to first be aware of your listening skills. Do you listen completely without starting to get defensive in your head? Being internal is the first step. You have to totally focus on what your significant other is saying instead of figuring out your comeback. If you can't figure out what they are saying, get clarification before becoming defensive. See if you can see the problem in the following scenario where there isn't any affirmation or validation.

John: "Honey, is something wrong? You seem distant."

Jaime: "That is ridiculous. Why would you think that?"

John: "I don't know."

Jaime: "Why do you always think something is wrong? For God's sake, John."

John: "I just miss talking to you. You are always doing something else."

Jaime: "Like what? What are you talking about?"

John: "You were staring out the window."

Jaime: "Really? So, arrest me. I'm in a no-stare zone."

John: "Just forget it. Stare all you want, I'm going upstairs."

You will see a big difference with the same situation when validation and affirmation are used.

John: "Honey, is there something wrong? You seem distant."

Jaime: "You think I'm distant?" (This is a sign of affirmation.)

John: "I noticed you were staring out the window."

Jaime: "I guess I was. If I were you, I'd probably think the same thing. (This is validation.) Nothing is wrong. I'm just enjoying the snow falling and thinking about when my parents used to take us sledding when we were kids."

John squeezes her hand: "I love watching the snow fall, too. Do you mind if I sit and watch with you?"

Validation and affirmation will take some practice. Focus on what your partner is saying, completely listen, and acknowledge you heard them by affirming what they said. "You think I should finish the dishes now." Ask some questions if you have to clarify what you heard. "What is bothering you? Is it the dishes sitting in the sink?" Never rush with a response. Validate. It isn't necessary to agree with your partner. You just need to validate they have a right to feel what they are feeling. "It doesn't matter if they sit there until we have walked the dog. I know clutter bothers you and you seem to be a bit frustrated. Is this it?"

These simple skills pack some power. When therapists introduce these to couples, they might discount them at first, resist following through, or feel awkward.

When talking about codependent relationships, there will be a bunch of stuff happening underneath the level of communication. It will be hard for some people to admit they don't understand how to talk to their significant other. When they come in for therapy, they are on guard about their partner's disapproval. It might be very uncomfortable for a person who is codependent to show their weakness during therapy. It might be hard for them to ask for what they want. The therapist is responsible for walking the line between therapy and teaching, between holding a person responsible and reassuring, especially if the client is codependent.

One Last Reminder Before Conclusion

Have you grabbed your free resource?

A lot of information has been covered in this book. As previously shared, I've created a simple mind map that you can use _right away_ to easily understand, quickly recall and readily use what you've learned in this book.

If you've not grabbed it...

Click Here To Get Your Free Resource

Alternatively, here's the link:

https://viebooks.club/freeresourcemind-mapforcodependency

Your Free Resource Is Waiting..

Get Your Free Resource Now!

Conclusion

Thank you for making it through to the end of this book. Let's hope it was informative and able to provide you with all the tools you need to achieve your goals, whatever they may be.

You have probably uncovered some things about yourself within these pages. You may have even uncovered some things about those in your life. This could leave you feeling confused or a little overwhelmed, but that's okay. Changing the way you do things in life can be frustrating, scary, and worthwhile. The important thing is to stick to what you have learned in this book. Use the methods that resonate with you the most.

Things won't change overnight. It will likely take you a while to make long-lasting changes. One thing is for certain, if you stick to these changes, your life will be better for it. Stick with your changes and don't second-guess why you are doing this. Trust me, you won't regret it.

Sincerely,

Margot Fayre

P.S.

If you've found this book helpful in any way, a review on Amazon is greatly appreciated.

This means a lot to me, and I'll be extremely grateful.

Notes

[1] Le Poire, BA. "Does the codependent encourage substance-dependent behavior? Paradoxical injunctions in the codependent relationship." *International Journal of Addiction* (1992): 1465-1474

[2] Hauge, L. J., Skogstad, A. and Einarsen, S. (2010). "The relative impact of workplace bullying as a social stressor at work." *Scandinavian Journal of Psychology*, 51: 426–433.

Related Books That Might Benefit You

Narcissistic Abuse Recovery in Toxic Relationship: Healing Love & Recovering from Covert Narcissism, Manipulation & Trauma - Dealing with Abusive Narcissist Partner, Family, Parent, Mother or Father

NARCISSISTIC ABUSE
RECOVERY IN
TOXIC RELATIONSHIP

Healing Love & Recovering from
Covert Narcissism, Manipulation & Trauma -
Dealing with Abusive Narcissist Partner,
Family, Parent, Mother or Father

NAILA FARRAH

This LIFE-CHANGING Guide Will Teach You How To Cut Narcissist Out Of Your Life So They Can Never Hurt You Again!

Do you often feel like you're condoning abusive behavior from people who claim to love you?

Have you stopped doing the things you love because someone in your life criticizes you for doing them?

Do you feel suffocated and overwhelmed because you are under constant undeserved scrutiny?

If you want to stop all these in your life, then keep reading...

Dealing with narcissists can be emotionally and psychologically exhausting and traumatic. Most narcissists feel entitled to everyone's attention, as well as exploit others without guilt or shame. Often times, the victims never really know what hit them until it's too late.

Award-winning author, Naila Farrah, knows a thing or two about falling victim to a narcissist. In fact, her experience was even more heartbreaking since the abuser was her own father — someone who is supposed to make her feel safe and loved. Once she had stopped condoning his bad behavior, her world changed for the better and this paved the way to her narcissistic abuse recovery. All of a sudden, it was like a heavy weight had been taken off her shoulders. She became happier, brighter, and content... and she wishes the same things for you, too!

In her book, Farrah aims to empower people like you to take back control and start living life free from toxic, controlling people.

***Narcissistic Abuse Recovery in Toxic Relationship*, the only book you'll ever need to discover the reality of covert narcissism and learn how to spot a narcissist with narcissistic personality disorder before they start hurting you!**

Here's a taste of what you'll discover inside *Narcissistic Abuse Recovery in Toxic Relationship*:

- ***Swiftly learn the signs to watch out for*** so you can SKILLFULLY stop a narcissist from coming into your life and creating chaos

- *Easily find out if you're in a relationship with a narcissist* so you can EFFECTIVELY deal with them and kick start your own narcissistic abuse recovery

- *Effectively cut toxic people out of your life* using this one FOOLPROOF method that will change the course of your life

- *Fast-track your healing from a narcissistic relationship* and get your life back in a snap using PROVEN techniques and tools

- *Discover the exact ways* you can QUICKLY heal your brain from all the emotional turmoil and trauma and reverse whatever damage has been done

- *Use SCIENCE-BACKED, practical advice* so you can FINALLY move forward and start a new life away from your narcissistic abuser

- *Immediately free yourself* from a narcissistic person's grip and start cultivating healthier relationships with a few SIMPLE steps

And much, much more...

If you're ready to finally learn how to deal with a narcissist, break free from the emotional and psychological chaos, start your narcissistic abuse recovery, and live a happier, contented and fulfilled life, now is the time.

Emotional Abuse Recovery: Men & Women Suffering in Silence – Emotionally Abusive, Destructive Relationship or Marriage with Manipulative, Toxic People (Healthy Healing and Recovering from Trauma)

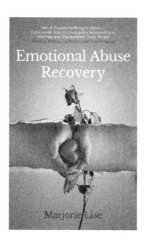

Stop Suffering In Silence & Finally Heal From Emotionally Abusive Relationship With The Help Of This POWERFUL Guide!

Are you constantly feeling emotionally tortured and betrayed by someone you used to love and adore?

Do you see no point in even trying to get out because your abusive partner has taken full control of your life?

Do you feel suffocated and helpless because it just seems like no one understands, or knows how to help you?

If you want to stop all these in your life, then keep reading...

Going through, and subsequently healing from emotional abuse is easier said than done. Most times, abuse victims feel blamed for staying or getting themselves into that kind of relationship in the first place.

Abuse survivor turned domestic violence advocate, Marjorie Lise, knows this story all too well. Lise had stayed with her abusive partner for an entire decade, before realizing that she deserved better. In her book, she talks about how she was able to successfully stop suffering in silence and finally escape her abuser, with the hope that her experience will inspire others to take back control of their lives, too.

Lise wants people like you to know that there is HOPE!

Emotional Abuse Recovery, the only book you'll ever need to get out of an emotionally abusive relationship and finally start to heal!

Here's a taste of what you'll discover inside *Emotional Abuse Recovery*:

- *Unmistakable signs to watch out for* to accurately recognize and effectively address toxic relationships, manipulative people and emotional abusers

- *Destructive ways that emotional manipulation* can affect a person for the rest of their life

- *Detailed and clear guidelines in taking the first steps* in dealing with your abuser, starting the healing process, and taking back control of your life

- *Proven methods in creating an air-tight safety plan* that will help you get out of EVERY sticky, abusive situation

- *Effective techniques to maximize the positive effects* that guided journaling can do in easing negative emotions stemming from abuse

- *Actionable tips that help you be and stay strong during the critical recovery stage*, so you won't feel the need to give in or go back to your abuser ever again

- *Highly reliable, helpful, and easily accessible resources* that you can use whenever you need emotional, physical, and mental help

And much, much more...

If you're ready to finally heal from your trauma, experience emotionally healthy relationships that you deserve, and say goodbye to your abusive torturer for good, now is the time.

Did My Narcissistic Mother Love Me?: Dealing with Manipulation & Trauma from Narcissist - Healing & Recovery of Narcissism Abuse in Toxic, Abusive Family Relationship with Parents, Mother or Father

Discover The PROVEN, Most Effective Ways To Heal From Abusive, Narcissistic Mothers & FINALLY Thrive In Life & Relationships!

Are you feeling overwhelming resentment and anger towards your narcissistic mother and some of your family members?

Do you struggle with regulating your emotions and letting other people in?

Do you feel frustrated because you can't seem to find a way to heal from your emotional wounds and establish healthy, loving relationships with others?

If you want to stop all these in your life, then keep reading...

One of the most difficult things for wounded children to accept is the fact that there is a very small chance that their narcissistic mothers will ever change. At best, they will look for ways to address their toxic traits and grow for the better. However, narcissists *rarely change*... and if they do start acting nicer, more often than not, it's because they seek to manipulate.

Award-winning author and narcissistic abuse survivor, Nanette Abigail, knows a thing or two about this sensitive issue. Her own experience with getting out of a controlling relationship with her mother equipped her with the insider knowledge, that had allowed her to finally wake up to the reality that the problem wasn't her, and that what she went through wasn't her fault.

In her book, Abigail lays out the crucial tools she used to set boundaries, create safe havens, and find mental clarity for herself... and with her help, you can, too!

***Did My Narcissistic Mother Love Me?*, the only book you'll ever need to heal and move forward with life after suffering emotional turmoil from narcissistic parents.**

Here's a taste of what you'll discover inside *Did My Narcissistic Mother Love Me?*:

- *7 Essential facts adult daughters* with a narcissistic family need to be aware of, so they can FINALLY see and accept the hard truth

- ***Expert-approved methods to iden-tify that VITAL moment*** your Psychological Immune System starts kicking in and field-tested ways to effectively boost it

- ***Eye-opening insights to understand WHY*** you grieve for the loving mother you never had, so you can finally start to overcome your negative emotions and destructive attachment

- ***Important first steps to kick off the process of healing*** from the toxic, narcissistic relationship you have with your abusive mother

- ***Proven ways to deal with your anger***, so you can clearly understand the reality of the situation you were in as you start your narcissistic abuse recovery

- ***Foolproof techniques to skillfully detach from and set healthy boundaries*** with a mother consumed with narcissism

- ***Practical tips in maximizing healing benefits*** of mindfulness as you recover from your abusive parents

And much, much more...

If you're ready to finally learn how to deal with, set healthy boundaries, heal from your narcissistic mother, and say goodbye to the overwhelming feelings of helplessness, now is the time.

Printed in Great Britain
by Amazon

73205467R00122